Charge

In his ~~first book~~ (*Psychic Power* *101*), renowned psionics expert Charles Cosimano showed thousands of people how to build simple, effective and inexpensive radionic devices that give you the ability to function in the psychic world with greater efficiency. Now he is back with a new book that reveals even more astounding information that will make you a psychic Power Master.

Psionic Power picks up where *Psychic Power* left off, guiding you deeper into the technology of psychic power. *Psychic Power* taught you the basic skills: how to make thoughtforms, pendulums and radionic boxes. *Psionic Power* explains how and why these machines work and gives more advanced techniques for creating and amplifying psychic power.

Psionic Power is the only book of its type in the field. It fuses ancient magick and modern technology into a workable whole. The machines in this book give you the chance to greatly expand your native psychic ability with much less work than the more traditional schools of psychic teaching would require, thus reducing the tendency to failure. It is not exaggerating to say that literally everyone can do some of the things in this book, and most can do them all.

To those who are new to the subject, this book will still serve as a complete guide. Equipment described in the first book is given in the Appendix. This makes it perfect for those who missed the first book, while guiding the veteran onward.

You may have tried any number of systems for developing psychic abilities and had little success. Psionic Power is a system that works.

About the Author

Charles W. Cosimano has been a teacher of psychic and magickal skills for more than ten years. He has an M.A. in History. More recently his interests have led him to become an active researcher and writer. He is a member of Phi Alpha Theta fraternity, and is the past chairman and current secretary of the Wheaton, Illinois, Study Center of the Theosophical Society in America, where he shares his home with two cats.

To Write to the Author

We cannot guarantee that every letter written to the author can be answered, but all will be forwarded. Both the author and the publisher appreciate hearing from readers, learning of your enjoyment and benefit from this book. Llewellyn also publishes a bi-monthly news magazine with news and reviews of practical esoteric studies and articles helpful to the student, and some readers' questions and comments to the author may be answered through this magazine's columns if permission to do so is included in the original letter. The author sometimes participates in seminars and workshops, and dates and places are announced in *The Llewellyn New Times*. To write to the author, or to ask a question, write to:

Charles W. Cosimano
c/o THE LLEWELLYN NEW TIMES
P.O. Box 64383-096, St. Paul, MN 55164-0383, U.S.A.

Please enclose a self-addressed, stamped envelope for reply, or $1.00 to cover costs.

ABOUT LLEWELLYN'S NEW AGE PSI•TECH SERIES

Psychic Powers—we really understand very little about them. But, with an open mind, we have to admit the evidence that they do exist. We witness them in history, religion and myth, and we witness them all about us in both ordinary and extraordinary circumstances. We witness these amazing powers in psychic phenomena, radionics and psionics, in divination and dowsing, in healing and prophecy, and in miracles and mysteries of all kinds.

Over the whole history of humanity, these powers have been experienced and cultivated by shamans, magicians, witches and yogis, by holy (whole) men and women, and by people-in-need. Today, we also find them in the research laboratory and in the homes and offices of ordinary men and women seeking understanding of such phenomena and powers so that they can be directed and applied to self-improvement and attainment, *and for success.*

There are many *technologies* for developing and applying these little-known powers. But even when we lack understanding of how something works, we can still find ways to apply it for our own benefit. Psychic Power lies dormant in everyone, and everyone—no matter who he or she is—can bring it out and use it. There are established technologies for psychic development and application, and there are simple "machines" (or interfaces) that can help develop and amplify your psychic powers.

In Llewellyn's Psi•Tech Series of books and tapes, we focus on these techniques and devices for tapping the many powers of the psyche, including those that join psyche and body, visible and invisible, life and Earth, humanity and cosmos. With this knowledge we seek better control over the personal environment, adding a new and significant resource in dealing with the problems of everyday living—*and a means to understand and control the invisible factors that shape energies and events at community and planetary levels.*

Other Books by Charles W. Cosimano

Psychic Power

Forthcoming

Psionic Warfare amd Self-Defense
The Psionic Gadget Cut-Out Book
Psionic Magick

Llewellyn's New Age Psi•Tech Series

Psionic Power

The High Technology of Psychic Power

Charles W. Cosimano

1989
Llewellyn Publications
St. Paul, Minnesota 55164-0383, U.S.A.

International Standard Book Number: 0-87542-096-6
Library of Congress Catalog Number: 89-2488

First Edition, 1989
First Printing, 1989

Library of Congress Cataloging -in-Publication Data
Cosimano, Charles W., 1949-
    Psionic power / by Charles W. Cosimano.
        p. cm.—(Llewellyn's new age psi-tech series)
    Bibliogrphy: p.
    ISBN 0-87542-096.6 : $3.95
    1. Psychical research. 2. Occultism. I. Title. II. Series
BF 1031.C63 1989   89-2488
133.8—dc19   CIP

Cover Painting by Martin Cannon
Illustrations by Christopher Wells

Produced by Llewellyn Publications
Typography and Art property of Chester-Kent, Inc.

Published by
LLEWELLYN PUBLICATIONS
A Division of Chester-Kent, Inc.
P.O. Box 64383
St. Paul, MN 55164-0383, U.S.A.
Printed in the United States of America

Contents

WELCOME BACK

For those of you who were fortunate enough to have read my first volume, *Psychic Power** (which is, incidentally, not to be confused with the infamous Room 101 of George Orwell), I feel an obligation to explain that this work is going to be a bit different. Yes, it will have the same biting wit and fascinating repartee, but this book is going to be just a little harder to understand, because, while in my first volume I was primarily concerned with teaching my readers how to make such useful things as thoughtforms, pendulums and radionic boxes, this book will explain (at least in some greater detail than in *Psychic Power*) why the methods introduced in the first volume work, and will introduce a few more advanced techniques. In addition, I will try to dive into waters in which most researchers fear to swim by commenting on research methods and even the ethics (or non-ethics) thereof.

But enough of this merriment, as the inquisitor said to his victim. Let us begin with a consideration of one of the most difficult problems facing any student in the field of the psychic—language—for no matter how important what we have to say is, it will not matter one

---

* originally titled *Psionics 101*.

bit if no one can understand what we are talking about. This fact should be obvious to everyone with the exception of social scientists and bureaucrats.

Montague Summers, that most credulous and hostile chronicler of things occult and arcane, once began a work by quoting some advice given by a well-known (at least to his students) tutor at Oxford. That worthy gentleman never missed the opportunity to remind his students to "define your terms." I will set aside my midwestern prejudice against all things British and follow that adage by trying to make some sense out of the words used to describe our study.

Some of the words under which the material I will cover are clearly inappropriate. *Occult* and *supernatural* are the most obvious. Occult means "hidden," and if it is available to the general public at any bookstore it is certainly not that; and supernatural is impossible. There is no such thing as the supernatural, there is only that part of nature that we do not yet understand. For example, to the most knowledgeable person in the fifteenth century, television would have been supernatural. Now it is merely annoying. Or, to give a more modern example, the flight of the bumblebee is impossible according to the classical theories of aerodynamics. All this means, however, is that there is an error in the theory somewhere, and the specialist in that field does well to discover it before he or she gets stung.

Finding things with a rod or a pendulum used to be commonly called divining, and it still is in some quarters. That term has gone out of fashion because of a number of factors. For one thing, we do not now believe that the art is the result of divine intervention.

It has popularly been replaced by "dowsing," which is as good a word as any, provided you are not near a swimming pool. Its meaning is limited to finding information by psychic means with the aid of some simple instrument.

The French, with their love of making the simple complex, coined the term *radiesthesia*, which literally means "distant sensing." This word has two strikes against it. First, it only refers to gathering information, which is only one part of what we are doing. Second, and this I admit is something of a personal bias, is that the word itself sounds like something you would hear under less than comfortable circumstances. Imagine yourself lying in the hospital, watching your soap opera, when in comes someone in a white coat who says, "Hi! I'm Bobby, your radiesthesist." And before you can say "I'M ONLY IN FOR TESTS!" you are on the operating table, donating a kidney to someone you do not even like.

Radionics might at first glance seem like the perfect term. It implies not only the gathering of information by psychic means but also acting by those means. Of course *magick* covers the same verbal territory, but that word is encumbered by tons of mumbo-jumbo and social prejudice. Radionics seems to sound almost respectable. Unfortunately, radionics refers to a very specific form of psychic activity, which virtually requires the use of certain instruments with nice dials and numbers. There are those who wish to expand the meaning of the term and break out of that mold, but it must be admitted that they have served to cause more confusion than knowledge.

It is due to the weakness of the other terms that I

have chosen to use the word *psionics*. I admit that it too has it deficiencies. Psionics has a certain science-fictiony tone to it, which is hardly surprising, as it was coined by two science-fiction writers, John W. Campbell and E. E. Smith. It also creates a certain confusion on the part of those who are not familiar at all with the terminology of the field and when told that a book is about psionics return a blank stare and ask, "What's that?" But these difficulties aside, I find it to be the perfect word for all device-assisted psychic activity, much better, for example, than the term coined by Christopher Hills, *supersensonics*, if only that it is much less of a mouthful to pronounce.

To put it another way, radiesthesia is sensing at a distance. Radionics is defined as acting at a distance. Radiesthesia, plus radionics, plus psychic development in general, equals psionics.

THE JOY OF POWER

I hope that my little digression did not annoy you too much. For with that out of the way, we can get busy and start making you a true adept at psionics.

Before we begin, however, I should point out that this is the second volume of a series on the subject, and much of the material contained is a continuation of the material in my first book, *Psychic Power*. But do not let that deter you. There will be a great deal of material in this one that does not need the background of the other book, and the equipment mentioned in the first book is explained in Appendix 4. Therefore, if you have not had the good fortune of reading *Psychic Power*, I recommend that you begin with that appendix and build the pendulum, radionic box and psionic amplifying helmet, as well as the teleflasher. These are basic tools and you will profit much by the exercise.

Assuming, however, that you are among the lucky many who have studied my previous work, you may begin to use this book in earnest, and it is well to begin with a good, honest look at yourself and your view of the world around you. This may seem like strange advice with which to start off a book on psionics, but it is very important, far more important than I realized when I wrote my first book. If you will recall, I told you in that work that you should not be afraid of having and using power. I explained that power is nothing more than the ability to accomplish your ends, irrespective of the nature of those ends. Well, my friend, there is more to it than that.

All psychic functioning, no matter how sugarcoated its advocates like to make it, is designed for the sole purpose of giving its user the capacity to accomplish things that he or she might not otherwise be able to accomplish. It also gives the user an advantage in the great struggle of life, for as Thomas Hobbes said, "Man is wolf to Man," to which a dentist friend of mine has added, "And the wolf with the best teeth wins!"

This simple fact of existence drives some people absolutely nuts. And, as you can well imagine, those who are unwilling to recognize life as consisting mainly of struggle and conflict are going to have a very bad time in using psychic power, with or without the aid of psionic devices, to achieve anything.

You must be willing to understand that guilt is an emotion, and it can be a most pernicious emotion at that. Every time you set it off, you put out a certain amount of energy, and if you do that often enough you are inevitably going to create a thoughtform that will draw disaster to yourself. In effect, your conscience will be doing to you what no outside force is able to.

So it is really very important that you be able to function with psychic energy and not feel guilty about doing so. And you must also not feel guilty about gaining results from that activity, and that can be the harder part.

Now I am not asking you to give up your conscience entirely. What I am asking you to do is to take a good look at the world around you and realize that there are times in life when what we do not want is a fair chance. Rather, what we want is to be able to stack the deck.

There is also the added element of freedom. I am a strong believer in the freedom of the individual to pursue his or her destiny, and there are times when in the pursuit of that freedom it will be necessary to step on someone else's foot. If you are going to grow, if you are going to evolve, you are going to have to do whatever is necessary to maximize that freedom without which nothing else is worth having. Psionics can do that for you. It can give you those abilities that are necessary to stack the deck in your favor. It is all very well to speak of cooperation, but what is being worked with here is a fundamentally individualistic system, and if you cannot act as an individual, then you are going to be little use to any group you may wish to help. To those who use the Christian command, "Love thy neighbor as thyself," I offer the reminder that it is necessary to love thyself first.

Once you have mastered that element, then you may work with others if you wish. Cooperation is often useful but only when it occurs with a primary respect for the individuals involved in the effort. Nothing lasting or of value is ever achieved by people acting as a flock of sheep, mindlessly following their leader or guru into some idealistic never-never land. No, what you must do is stand first on your own legs and be responsible for your own actions.

In psionics you are only responsible to yourself,

and that is quite enough. You do not have to justify either your interests in this area or your actions to anyone else. But you must be willing to face the results of those actions, and if you get something you did not quite plan on, to not go around blaming other people.

You must also understand and accept that the methods I am teaching fall under the heading of what is sometimes called Practical Occultism. By that I mean that you are working for mundane ends, not spiritual growth. The growth will come, for it comes with any increase in knowledge, but it is not the real purpose of this work. You will not attain enlightenment by psionics. And it is important that you do not fall into a common trap.

Often individuals will develop a psychic ability and with that ability an ego to match. They assume that because they have this new skill they have climbed a long way on some spiritual ladder, when all they have done is learn to use an ability, a skill, that anyone can use. Please do not make that mistake.

Just because you may feel that you have the secrets of the universe at your beck and call does not mean that you will serve any purpose by rubbing that fact into everyone you meet. It is best to keep quiet about these matters, for not everyone is enthused about the possibility of being the unwitting subject of a psychic experiment, especially when that experiment may cause them some personal difficulty. One of the rules about the use of power of any type, and psychic power most especially, is that those who truly have it do not need to make a show of it. Now I know that it can be very tempting to show off your new abilities, and I will confess that when I was young and foolish I did the same thing. But in the end that sort of behavior serves no purpose other than to have those who dislike us, usually out of jealousy, get a good laugh when something goes wrong.

The truth of the matter is that a laugh enjoyed in secret can very often be much more satisfying than one enjoyed in public. There is no point in going out of our way to make enemies. We can do that just by normal living.

Of course, psionics can give you a tremendous advantage if you should make an enemy, or even if you are faced with a problem that might otherwise create a great deal of hard feelings if an attempt to solve it were allowed to take the normal course of screaming, yelling, fistfights and lawsuits. So let me explain that advantage with an example.

Some years ago one of our neighbors had the bad luck to be afflicted with several offspring, and due to undoubtedly bad management on his part, they grew into late adolescence. As if this were not a bad enough situation, one of them, in spite of much good counsel from his elders, decided that he had an ear for music and wished to make his fortune as a rock musician. To make matters worse he formed a band and was using his father's garage for a practice site. The result was that I and the rest of my neighbors were fervently wishing for a nuclear attack to restore peace and quiet to our lives. They were even drowning out low-flying jets! To add to my difficulties was the fact that I actually liked the neighbor. He was and is a good, honest person who on many occasions has helped me push my car out of the snow. He is always ready to loan his tools and is full of advice on the arcane mystery of killing crabgrass. So hiring a gangster to kill off his children was not what is termed a "viable solution."

It was at this point in time that I began experimenting with what is termed a disruption pattern (I will explain them in full later), and thus I used a radionic device transmitting such a pattern at the band. After a few days of this, during which I wondered if the machine were actually going to work, I discovered that a strange, almost indefinable something had descended on the neighborhood. For the first night in two months it was actually quiet.

What had happened? Had my neighbor come to his senses and shipped his son off to the merchant marine? No, the answer was much simpler than that. Another neighbor, who was on less good terms with the family of the budding musician (and I use the term very loosely indeed) had summoned various attendant spirits in the form of the local police to annoy, harrass and otherwise persuade the source of the racket that his efforts were not appreciated. Thus, any opprobrium was on that neighbor and not me, and I was able to go back to my research and the summer reruns in peace, while the other neighbor, who had been influenced by my machine, found himself in the middle of an unwanted feud, which by now has peacefully ended.

You see how useful this stuff could be. And you also see the value of keeping your mouth shut. Suppose I had run around the town telling everyone that I was zapping the band? The advantage of the secret transmission would have been completely lost, if not worse. One of the advantages of psionics is that one is able to live a life without fear, and secrecy is one of the keys to retaining that state.

There is another way to enjoy psionics and the power it brings, and that is in the playing of little pranks. In my last book I got into a bit of trouble with some of my readers who were a little disturbed by one small exercise that involved visualizing a drill boring into the back of somebody's neck. I confess that I expected some of my ideas to raise the hairs on a few heads, but I was really surprised that that one method would create such a response. It seemed pretty harmless to me. After some thought I think I found the answer. It was not the experiment itself that bothered people, it was the idea of having fun with it. To most people who get very involved in psionics this is very serious material, not to be taken lightly or treated with irreverence.

Now I should not be too harsh on some of those who view with alarm anything that might detract from the seriousness with which they take their subject. Psionics has a very bad reputation in this country, and some have worked very hard to try to make it respectable, almost a new branch of physics. In doing so they get laughed at a lot, so when someone comes along who laughs at everything, well, they get a little intense.

But is anything served by that intensity? The answer is no. My demands are quite simple. All I expect of you is a little common sense. Realize that you have certain abilities, and don't be afraid to use them, no matter what people around you or other writers say. Face life without fear, and know that as you progress you will be more than a match for any slings, arrows or old bottles that outraged and outrageous fortune may see fit to hurl in your direction.

THE FIELD

As this is being written, it was ten years ago that the movie *Star Wars* popularized the idea of what in the film was called "The Force." The concept had been floating around for some time, but it was the movie that made the idea of an all-pervasive universal energy field that could be manipulated by those with the skill truly common.

While calling it The Force may have been good cinema, it was hardly accurate. What is really out there, at least what we think is really out there, is an energy field that interpenetrates everything. This field is the basic stuff of life itself, and it is, as I explained in my last book, the building material of matter itself. Just how this works is a subject of much conjecture, and I will never claim to have the last word on it, but a convenient explanation of how it functions goes something like this.

The field begins as a pure energy flow, from what source we cannot begin to guess, and continues until for some reason it is interfered with. This interference slows it down and in the process creates the ultimate in subatomic particles. Each particle has a polarity, and it is the nature of polarity to attract and repel. Thus the particles tend to grow. This particle we will term a *psion*, because it is a longstanding tradition that the names of subatomic particles have an ON at the end of their name. Let me admit that I have no way of proving that these particles actually exist, but if they do, it is a very convenient way of explaining certain things that happen in psychic work, such as the creation of thoughtforms.

A psion does not have to be created by the original energy wave. It may also come from electrical activity in the human brain. This fact would seem to have some very far-reaching implications, as the television commentators like to say, but we will not concern ourselves with them at the moment. Suffice it to say that this seems to be the reason why certain forms of psychic functioning and ability are influenced by the magnetic field of the Earth and by certain weather conditions, two things that one would expect not to matter at all. It also explains why certain radionic experiments are aided by the input of either electric current or light beams.

I have a confession to make at this point. I have long found discussions of magnetic fields and their relation to dowsing annoying. It did not make any sense to me that a function which one would assume would be purely a function of the human consciousness should be concerned in any way with the amount of humidity in the air, or the direction in which the dowser was standing, in spite of the tremendous amount of evidence to the contrary. I put it down to some weird failing in the psychology of the writers. Well, it is not the first time that I have been wrong. Clearly there is such an effect, and some have gone to great lengths to avoid problems that may result from it. Guyon Richards, an early radionic researcher, for example, would work inside a Faraday cage to insure that no stray electromagnetic field would disturb his findings. Obviously I do not expect you to go to such extremes. I do not.

This explains why the psionic amplifying helmet will sometimes work better when the wearer aligns him/herself north-south, and may even explain the problem of pyramid alignment. Of course it leaves us with another difficulty that may concern those who pick up this book in an antique shop some centuries from now, and that is what will people out in space do with no Terran magnetic field to work with. I hope I live to see dowsing experiments done in space so that I can study the results.

But enough of this technical stuff. Just bear in mind that there is a relation between psychic activity and electromagnetic energy, something akin to the relation between electromagnetic energy and torque.

Dr. Robert Massey has put together a number of laws on the practice of dowsing, which by extension may apply to all psionic devices and ultimately to all psychic activity. The most important is the first: "If it exists, it is known."[1] The assumption behind this principle is that anything that exists, or occurs, has a reflection in the consciousness of the universe. If the universal consciousness is aware of it, then the human consciousness can become aware of it by the proper tuning, either by direct knowledge or by the aid of instruments.

From this concept we may make another assump-

---

[1]Victor Beasley, *Your Electro-Vibratory Body.*

tion—that anything which exists can be studied and analyzed. There is nothing that humankind is not meant to know.

From analysis we can make a further statement. Anything that exists can be manipulated. Hence, as we can know about psychic energy, we can therefore study and analyze it, and as we do that, we learn how to put it to work for us.

So let's start putting this stuff to work. We will begin by using the stuff we learned in studying *Psychic Power*—meditation and visualization.

As you already know, you have an energy body surrounding and interpenetrating your physical one. This we call the etheric body (see Figure 1). In my first book I simply lumped all the functions of your energy body into the etheric body, and I did this for the sake of simplicity. Actually, it gets a little more complex. Your etheric body has a number of gradations within it, and these gradations each have different functions.

Closest to your body is your aura. This is the segment that shows up in Kirlian photography and other aura-seeing methods, such as the Kilner glasses. It is the densest level of the etheric body, aside from the physical body itself. The colors that are sometimes seen in this aura reflect various aspects of the personality and health of the person. At times, waveforms and thoughtforms are also picked up by those who are sensitive to such things, though these usually appear at the next level, which is the etheric body proper. It is less dense than the aura and is rarely visible except to certain extraordinarily gifted individuals. It is at this level that most waveforms and thoughtforms that can affect the health of the physical body are found.

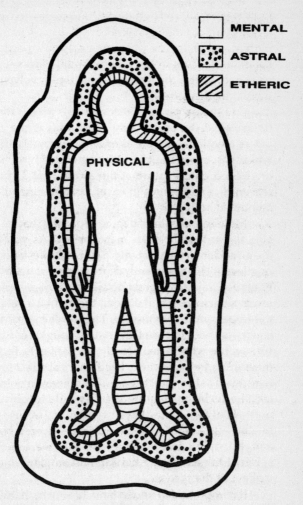

Figure 1

The etheric body is the stuff which the physical body is hung on, and it contains those somewhat mysterious vortices called chakras. I will discuss these in more detail later. The phenomenon known as kundalini also occurs in the etheric body. Most psionic work that affects the physical body will involve manipulating this level.

Of a somewhat less dense nature is what is sometimes called the astral body. This level is the area where emotional responses have their greatest effect, and it is sometimes stated that emotions have their origin and entire nature at the astral level. For that reason it is sometimes more accurately termed the emotional body.

Moving to the finest degree of density that we are able to work with is the mental body. As you can guess, all intellectual activity has its manifestation at this level. The nineteenth-century writers who delighted in going into great detail about these various levels went further and divided the mental level into the upper and lower mental. The lower mental was concerned with the usual everyday thoughts of a person, such as what to make for dinner, while the higher mental level was concerned with more abstract problems, such as how much to tip after dinner. In point of fact, the distinction is quite arbitrary and probably has no basis in fact. It may have been put in because the human was supposed to have a seven-layered body, and when you take out the two that were purely spiritual in nature, you have to add an extra one to make it fit the system.

It is important to understand, however, that all of these levels continually interact with each other and none is completely independent. They also are continually influencing and are influenced by the physical body, which by the normal five senses picks up and transmits to them the information that causes the various reactions in each body.

It's example time again. Let us assume that you are having a reasonably good day, with no more than the usual disasters. Then the mail comes, in the morning for a change. You go to the door and bring it in, separating your own mail from that of the neighbors, which has been delivered to you by mistake, and seeing that one of the envelopes is undoubtedly a bill, you open it. At this point your good day turns into a very bad one indeed, for the company has billed you several thousand dollars for something that should only have been $13.95.

As your brain processes this information, the message goes to the mental level, which literally screams ERROR, and screams it so loud that the astral, or emotional level, which had been more or less dozing, wakes up and begins to go berserk—or rather, you go berserk. The emotional message is transmitted back to your etheric body, which sends a message to your adrenal glands to begin pumping, and your heart rate starts to take off like a rocket. Speaking of rockets, your aura is taking on the appearance of a fireworks display, full of nice reds and blacks all blasting merrily off around your body. At this point the clairvoyant next door comes over to borrow a cup of sugar, takes one look at you, drops the cup and runs home in terror to have a heart attack.

You go to the telephone, dial the company number and get the billing manager, frantically demanding an explanation of the mistake. The billing manager is used to such small problems and is thus not as upset as you. After all, it is not his money. He calmly explains that the error was the result of an incompetent computer operator, who has since been fired.

Your brain transmits this information to your mental level, which in turn passes it along to your emotional level, which tells the etheric body to turn off the adrenalin; and your aura begins to take on a more normal coloring, which is of great comfort to the clairvoyant next door, who sees you just as she is being carried into the paramedic truck.

This is, I will admit, an extreme example, but you can see from it how the various levels of the etheric and physical bodies interact. With psionic devices, we can isolate the function at each level and influence it, thus allowing ourselves a great deal of control over our subjects.

Another feature of the various levels is the fact that while they all interpenetrate, the finer levels are more spread out from the physical level. So now we can do our first experiment.

For this experiment you will need the following objects:

- One subject, preferably human
- The radionic box described on pages 163–164 of *Psychic Power* (see pages 191–197 of this book for condensed instructions on building your own).
- A patch cable, such as used to connect that box to the psionic amplifying helmet (see pages 200–206 in the back of this book).
- A table
- A large sheet of paper

Lay the paper down on the table and seat your subject at one end of the table, laying his or her hand (either one will do) on the paper. Set your box on the table as far from the hand as the length of the cable will allow. Now write "etheric body" on a small piece of paper and place it in the can of the box. Take a rate for the etheric body of your subject. Now move the box a little closer to your subject so that you can rub the stick pad while holding the one end of the patch cable to a finger of your subject. Plug the other end of the cable into the left-hand jack on the box.

While slowly moving the end of the cable away from the finger, rub the stick pad and continue to do this until you get a stick. This point will be the extent of the etheric body from that finger. Repeat this procedure going around the hand and connect the points. The drawing that results will be a picture of the subject's etheric body. Of course, the etheric body extends in all directions from the physical, and there is some debate as to whether or not it forms an egg, a sphere, or a rough outline of the physical body itself. These minor details are really of very little importance to you, and so if you should run into the varying descriptions given on this subject, do not be overly concerned. Psionics is still something of an inexact science, which causes some annoyance to all of us who work with it, but it is a fact that cannot be ignored.

Once you have a drawing of the etheric hand, you should try to get the astral, or emotional, hand. This may prove to be a bit difficult, as the emotional body tends to expand or contract with the amount of energy being put into it. Therefore, with your subject as calm, or at least as happy, as possible, repeat the procedure, only this time set up the box for the emotional body. With any luck you should get another drawing, but do not be surprised if you run out of paper or even table. The astral level can extend quite far, even covering an entire house.

It is doubtful that you will be able to draw the mental level, unless you have a very large table and lots of paper. What you can do is to set the box for the rate for the subject's mental body and walk back from him or her, while rubbing the plate, always keeping the idea in mind that you will get a stick once you reach the limit of that body. Do not be surprised if you find yourself in another room when the stick occurs. I remember the first time I tried this experiment I found myself in my girlfriend's backyard, in the snow, without a coat. Needless to say, I advised her not to think so much, at least while I was doing this experiment.

What this small activity will teach you is just how far-reaching your energy body is under normal circumstances. Given the proper stimulation, it is possible to extend these bodies, particularly the astral and mental, even further.

Reset the box for the emotional body. Now have your subject think of something dreadful that has happened to him/her recently, preferably something that does not involve you. Once he/she is good and upset, begin measuring the distance that the astral body extends. You will find it to be quite a bit larger than when he/she was just sitting.

The same is true of the mental body. The more energy that is put into a body, the larger it becomes. Think of all the people on a crowded street, with all their physical bodies touching at various unwanted places, and then think of what it must look like if one were able to see the continuous intermingling of the various energy bodies. It is enough to make one quite frightened of crowds but for a simple fact. Most people have so little in common that the nature of their bodies is such that they can bang into each other without the physical brain even registering the contact. When it does, the result is a feeling of unease that can turn into claustrophobia. There are individuals who are so sensitive to such contact that they cannot sit near even their closest family without being uncomfortable. This is not a cultural matter. It is true that different societies have a different tolerance for closeness, and we Americans need a lot of space compared to the rest of the world, but the discomfort caused by the intermingling of energy bodies is something quite different. It is not a learned response but rather quite instinctive.

Of course, given the right amount of energy it is possible for the energy field of any individual to influence another person. Surely you have had the bad luck to be in a room where someone has been really hopping mad. It feels like somehow the air pressure in the room has suffered a dramatic and unhealthy increase. By now I am sure that you can figure out for yourself what has happened. The anger of the person has been translated into a marked increase in both the size and power of the emotional body. What you are feeling is not a physical sensation at all but rather a psychic one, which has been translated by your brain into the only response your nervous system is designed to handle. As I said before, it is possible to so expand this body that it can fill an entire house, so if you get absolutely furious, you can make every person in the home uncomfortable without leaving your room or even saying a word.

It is useful to be able to measure these bodies, not only in the amount of area that they cover but also in the energy level that they are functioning at. This is usually done by using a pendulum and a scale divided off between zero and 100. But I have found that there is an even better method.

You will need nothing more for this little device than a sheet of posterboard and a paper fastener with some scissors and drawing tools, such as ruler and compass.

Begin by cutting the posterboard so that it will be about the size of an ordinary piece of typing paper, $8\frac{1}{2}$ inches by 11 inches. Lay the piece of posterboard that you have cut so that the long side is horizontal to you, and then draw a ten-inch line about an inch up from the bottom. Mark the center of the line.

Now use the compass to draw a half circle over the line from one end to the other. Decrease the radius of the compass by about a half inch, and make another half circle inside the first.

Use the ruler to find the center of the half circles, which will be directly over the center of the line. Mark this with a line between the two half circles. Number this line 50.

With the base line at left being zero, divide the left half of the circles between zero and 50 by making equal spaces numbered 10, 20, 30, 40. Now repeat the process on the right side, from 50 to 100, 100 being the right base line.

Further divide each space with smaller marks

from one to nine. This will give you an easy-to-read scale of zero to 100.

Punch a hole at the center of the base line and cut out a strip of posterboard from the hunk left over to make a pointer. Cut one end of that strip to make a point. Punch a hole in the other end of the strip and then use a pencil to darken the point. Fasten the strip to the scale.

Okay, now that you have your gauge, are you ready for another experiment? What do you mean, "No"? This one is just as easy as the last one and not as much work. At least you will not have to move around so much, and there is no danger of you backing off the front steps.

Find your subject again. Now this time, instead of measuring the size of his or her bodies, you are going to measure the amount of energy in them. Sounds simple. And it is. Have your subject hold the probe wire and take the rate for his/her aura this time. Now set the gauge in front of you (it is not necessary to attach it to the box in any way), and place the pointer at zero. You should not get a stick there when you rub the pad, because if you do, that means your subject is probably dead. You will also not likely get a reading of 100, for that is the theoretical maximum point that anybody can reach and still be human.

With that out of the way, you can begin to take a measurement. Set the pointer between zero and ten and ask if the level of the aura is in that range. Do not expect a stick yet, as this is a very low range and a healthy subject rarely reads in it. Repeat the process for each ten points until you get a stick, let us say between 60 and 70.

Set the pointer at 63 and ask if the measurement is between 60 and 65. If you do not get a stick on your machine, set the pointer again, this time at 68, and ask again. This time your thumb stops. So put the pointer at 65 and move it one number at a time until you get a stick, let us say at 66. You know now that your subject's aura has a functional strength of 66 percent of theoretical maximum.

By this point you have probably figured out that all of our measurements, including the all-important rates, are mere arbitrary conventions. Therefore, if somewhere along the line one system of numbering seems inappropriate to you, you should have no qualms about changing it.

You may now repeat the procedure with each of the other bodies until you have a series of measurements that will give a pretty good idea of the overall condition of your subject. For example, if your subject is weak at the level of the mental body, it may be that he/she is not at his/her best thinking capacity that day. As time and practice goes by, you will be able to interpret your findings with great accuracy.

But how does this knowledge directly benefit you? After all, I promised to give you more information on meditation and visualization, and then I lead you on a merry romp measuring your friends' various energy fields and making you build a new gadget.

All kidding aside, you will need to know how to do these things in order to measure your own progress. It is terribly frustrating to be working at a visualization and not know if you are getting any results.

We are now going to teach you how to mold your etheric body for various purposes. This is not always as easy as it may sound. Some writers have suggested that you visualize while looking at yourself in the mirror. It sounds good, but it is very difficult to do. I know, because I spent years trying and never got anywhere with it. A far better method is to simply imagine yourself as you were taught to in my last book. Think of your aura, that part of the etheric body which is closest to your physical one. Try to see that aura in your mind. Do not worry about color or anything else for the moment—simply hold the idea of your aura in your mind and know that the aura is there. Now expand your image of yourself to the level of the etheric. Realize that the etheric body is as much a part of you as the physical and the aura.

Move your awareness now to the level of the mind itself, the mental body. Here is all your thinking capacity and processes by which you think. There is relatively little data stored here, most of that being kept available in the physical brain, but it is from here that the data is accessed and used. It is surprising that relatively few thoughtforms are found in the mental body, but the nature of the energies involved in thoughtform production usually place them in the astral body or the aura. The mental body is a very cold place, for no emotion at all is found here.

Now return your awareness to your physical body. Feel the incredible solidity of it and rejoice in that solidity. You are a physical being as well as, if not more than, a spiritual one, and you must enjoy your physical presence.

The purpose of that little guided tour was to give you a feel for what I have been talking about, for as you will remember from my last book, I feel that in the realm of the psychic there is no substitute for experience. Once you have looked into each body you will know what the body does, and perhaps more importantly, what it does not do.

Now you are going to repeat one of your experiments, using yourself as the subject. Take a picture* of yourself and put it into the sample can. Once you have done that, take a rate for your aura. Set your gauge at zero and begin stroking the pad. As soon as you have the distance you will get a stick. Repeat the experiment with each body until you have a series of measurements to start with. Then go back to the aura rate and measure the strength of each body. Be certain to record all of these measurements. This will give you a base from which you may determine the effectiveness of your work.

Once you have done this, reset the machine for your astral body. Begin to meditate, and while meditating, let your memory wander back to some emotionally charged incident in your life, happy or unhappy. Hold onto the memory and let it fill up all the available space in your astral body so that it seems that all your emotional capacity is dedicated to that moment in time. Now pull back to Earth, and using the gauge, measure both the size and strength of your astral body. You have a much larger figure for both, don't you?

Once you do this experiment, it is a good idea to meditate again, this time on something very calming, so that you will be fit for human company. Also, one

---

* This acts as a "witness," or "thing that represents" the actual subject of the experiment. A witness can also be a bit of handwriting, a ring usually worn by the subject, etc.

small word of warning. It is a bad idea to do this experiment when working with a partner. The emotions built up are very strong, and the results can be very unpleasant, if not downright dangerous, to anyone else in the room with you. I remember when I tried it, I held the image of some event that made me absolutely furious and I almost smashed some valuable furniture, so be careful. There are quite a few people out there who think we should all contact our most unpleasant memories, for whatever therapeutic value that may have. But there are some memories that are best kept repressed, and unless there should be an overwhelming reason not to, it is best to treat the worst experiences of our lives as sleeping tigers, to be walked carefully around and never kicked.

What you should learn from the above, aside from my warnings, is that it is possible to control the output of energy from the emotional body. In fact, that is the level which is most responsive to such changes. It is also the level that has the greatest impact on a subject whom you wish to influence. In spite of the more pervasive nature of the mental level, it is much easier to motivate a subject by producing an emotive response in him or her than by trying to put an abstract idea into the person's head.

In my last book I taught you how to use what is sometimes called the eye-beam. If you will recall, the procedure required that you focus the energy of your etheric body through your eyes to the target. Well, by using the astral body, one can attain some pretty significant results without even focusing on a specific target.

So now that you know this, let's have some truly

harmless fun. I am assuming that you have some capacity for self-control before you try this little trick, otherwise you might find yourself gaining a few pounds, so study yourself a little. And be honest! Can you get really hungry and hold off eating everything in sight? If you can, you are going to have a little fun the next time you go to a restaurant.

Before you walk into the restaurant, get yourself good and hungry. Be so hungry that if you did not have consummate self-control no one would have any food left on their plates. Feel the hunger gnawing its way into your astral body and feel the astral body expand as the feeling of hunger energizes it. Let the desire cause that body to expand until it fills an entire room, but control yourself and do not grab food off other people's plates as you are seated.

Now, while you are waiting for your own gargantuan repast, which you will have no trouble finishing, focus your thoughts on the solar plexus of somebody else in the room. The solar plexus is the spot where the response to emotion and the desire for food are greatest. That is where the term "gut feeling" comes from. Know that the person at the other table is feeling the desire and is responding to it.

At this point, the old principle of harmonics comes in. I am sure that you remember the old high-school physics demonstration of the two tuning forks, one set to humming and the other simply held. Remember what happened? The other fork began to hum at the same frequency as the other one, to the amazement of the class. Well you are doing the same thing to your subject's astral body. His or her emotions are responding to your hunger. Pretty soon he/she is going to be absolutely ravenous, and you will be able to tell when that point is reached when he/she starts devouring all the dinner rolls, in spite of the fact that they are at least four days old and some have little green spots. At that point, you may begin to work on the next subject, and soon the cook in the eatery will be working overtime and the management will be absolutely overjoyed at the sight of so many people enjoying their food. The diners, being so happy to have their bellies filled, will reward the waiters and waitresses with extra tips and everyone will be happy.

There is another aspect of the field that you should be aware of: that of color. To be honest with you, this is something that at times seems to be more trouble than it is worth, as there are a number of conflicting interpretations as to the meaning of certain colors in the aura, and, by extension, in the rest of the field. Color is, after all, nothing but the way the physical brain translates certain frequencies of light. We could just as well say that a person's field is showing certain wavelengths, but that would only confuse the issue more. Because of this it is very easy to dismiss the whole thing.

However, the detection of color in the etheric body, in particular at the levels of the aura and the astral body, can be of great use. Unfortunately, very few of us have the natural power of such detection, and it may be just as well that we do not have it. Those who do, often find that it only makes their lives even more difficult than they would normally be. Besides, with psionics there is no need to actually see the colors—one may study the aura and astral body with the aid of another simple device, the color disk.

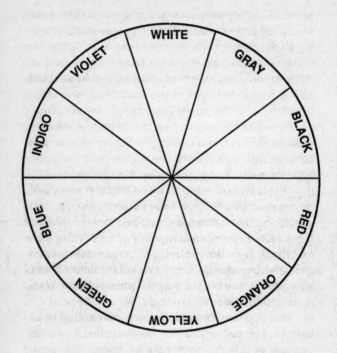

Figure 2

These disks can become quite complex, as various researchers have tried to use color to interpret everything from the aura to various minerals and elements. You should be content with a relatively simple one.

Make a copy of the disk in Figure 2. Be certain to get the colors in the same order, with gray the exact opposite of green. This is very important for reasons that I will explain later. Now make another pointer, as you did on your gauge, and cut out a sheet of poster-board the size of a piece of typing paper and glue the disk over it. Punch a hole in the center of the disk and at the flat end of your pointer. Attach the pointer to the disk with a paper fastener and you now have a color gauge.

You will notice that each color has a bit of area on the disk. The closer the pointer is to the center of a color wedge, the purer the color. This can be of some importance if you are making a detailed analysis of a subject, as you will have to in the near future.

So what do the colors mean? As I said, this is a subject of some controversy, so do not view my word as being completely authoritative on the matter. Experiment for yourself and see how your own mind interprets these things. The view I give you here is one that seems to fit most interpretations and is thus useful for most cases.

Black is a color you would not wish to find in an analysis of someone you like. It means that there is a deep malice, a serious wound that has never healed. Often seen as a slash across a red background by clairvoyants, it denotes great anger.

Red can mean anger. The purer the red, the greater the anger. It can also mean a person given to sensuality and thus can be a very difficult color for a clairvoyant to correctly interpret. All you have to do is ask your pendulum which it is.

Orange is a color that does not mean much. If it is strongly present, there is usually a very balanced personality. It is also the color associated with the flow of the vital force from the spleen chakra.

Yellow is a good color to have. It means the subject is smart. There are also those who say that a lot of yellow means the person has a highly spiritual nature. It is very difficult to make a determination in such matters, so the best thing to do is judge by the behavior of an individual. A spiritual-type person rarely beats his wife and children, no matter what platitudes he may repeat, while a person with a highly developed intellect will show it.

Green is another hard color to figure out. It may mean anything from cleverness to avarice.

Blue, on the other hand, is relatively easy to interpret. It almost always means a tendency to the mental as opposed to the physical. Hence a chessmaster has more blue in his aura than a basketball player, at least in general.

Indigo is usually mistaken for either blue or violet, so its presence can be a modification of the qualities of either. Those who emphasize the spiritual, as opposed to the mental, would think that the presence of indigo would mean a transition is taking place between the two.

Violet, on the other hand, is an almost purely spiritual color, and those who have a lot of it are usually heavenly minded. It is very rare to find anyone with this color in any great proportion.

Do not expect to find any white. It is almost never present in the aura or the astral body. But if you find gray, watch out, not only for the subject but also for yourself. Gray is a bad color to find in anyone because it tends to bring out, or perhaps show would be a better word, the worst aspects of the other colors.

Now that you have some idea what the various

colors can mean, you are going to do a little research. There is a little project that is sometimes given to students in beginning psychology courses, namely, to write what is called a "psychological profile" of someone, in which not only the behavior but the possible motivations of a person are analyzed. So pick a person you know well enough to study without his or her knowing it and write up such a profile. Consider everything you know about this person, how he/she reacts to various situations, how smart he/she is, his/her strengths and weaknesses (often the same thing in different contexts). Once you have done this, acquire a witness sample of the subject. This should be easy if you know him/her well enough.

Set up your machine and take a rate for his/her aura. Now place the color gauge and the number gauge in front of you and begin to look for colors. Place the pointer on each color and ask the stick pad if this color is present in the subject's aura. Write down each color that gives you a positive stick.

Once you have a list of the colors, write % on the paper next to the word "color." Your sheet will ultimately have three columns, and this is the second. Set the color dial again at each color you got a stick for, and ask the numerical gauge what percent of the aura is taken up by that color. Repeat this procedure for each color. By the way, do not be disturbed if your numbers do not quite add up to 100. There is constant fluctuation of color in the aura and astral body, so between each reading, as short a time as it is, the relative percentages will change. You are looking for a working approximation.

Now you may do the last part of this reading and

again set the pointer on the color disk at the first color. Write "intensity" on the paper in the third column. Take a numerical reading again for each color, with zero being the total lack of the color and 100 being the color making the aura literally glow.

The chart should look something like this.

Joe Doaks

Color	%	Intensity
Black	10	30
Red	25	10
Orange	5	10
Yellow	15	60
Blue	30	60
Gray	12	20

Now from this chart you can see right away that my friend Joe has a problem. There is only ten percent black, but it has an intensity of 30, which means that some deep hurt is still gnawing at him. Combine that with the presence of gray and you have a person who can be quite unhappy at times. Now Joe's profile says that he is given to fits of melancholy at times that can almost become depression, so that fits. You will notice that red is only 25 percent, while yellow and blue add up to 45 percent. That combined with the far greater intensity of blue and yellow over that of red means that Joe is a far more mental than physical person, and again that fits his profile. We also know that Joe has very little interest in anything spiritual, therefore we can assume that both yellow and blue in his case mean mental nature. The balancing factor of orange is five percent, and that means Joe has some small grasp on his problems but the combination of the other colors means that he is probably feeding his misery by thinking about it too much. We know from his profile that he is not in the habit of talking about his problems, like most of us, and therefore is keeping the fury bottled in. It is not dangerous at present, but any significant increase in either the gray or the black could mean that an explosion is imminent. Do not get this man drunk.

Well, now you have seen how it is done. You should repeat the procedure, first setting the radionic box for the subject's astral body. Doing this will give you an idea of the emotional makeup of the person you have chosen, and again, after you have finished, study the chart and compare the information with the data in his or her profile. This last is very important, for it can prevent you from making mistakes.

There is one man I know who has some clairvoyant abilities but has never learned to control them. He is too quick to make judgments based on incomplete data and is always giving people advice based on his spiritual studies and his visions.

This would not be a serious problem for this man if he would only take the time to learn something about the people he is talking to. Once he looked at my aura and decided that I could use some advice whether I wanted it or not. So he began doing an impromptu reading of my character from what he saw in my aura and naturally got everything wrong. For example, he told me that I was afraid of the dark. I should explain that due to a weird architectural fluke, my bedroom has no windows. Air comes in through vents aided by fans. Thus when I finally get to bed, about two or three on an average morning, it is quite impossible to find my hand without the aid of a flashlight. In fact, so used am I to this that I find it hard to sleep with any light at all coming in.

As you can imagine, I was less than impressed with both his information and his advice. If he had bothered to find out something about me first, he could have saved himself much embarrassment and trouble, to say nothing of being on the receiving end of my humor for the next year. And this was only because he was trying to be helpful.

Thus you have learned not only what to do, but also what not to do, which can be just as valuable. You will see this even more clearly as we go along.

As you now have some practice in the basic method of analysis, you are about to have the pleasure of applying that same skill to yourself. Remember, you cannot hope to influence other people unless you can control yourself, and the first rule is to know enough about yourself to have some idea where you are likely to run into a weak point. After all, if you know that a potential character weakness is present, you can act to compensate for it before anyone can take advantage of it.

Be ruthless with yourself in this matter. Remember, anything you may miss may very well be the heel where the arrow hits. Begin by making a profile of yourself. Do not underestimate or overestimate any weakness or strength. Once you have done this, study the colors of your aura and astral body and compare that information with your profile. Do not be afraid to admit to yourself that you have some quality that needs work.

Let me give you another example. I have one quality that works both as a strength and as a weakness. I have been blessed with the ability to be totally oblivious to the feelings of other people. Often, I do not even recognize their physical presence. This is the sort of thing you must look for. The more you know, the less you can be surprised.

Once you gain this information, what do you do? First determine if what you think is a weakness really is one, so you look not only at your profile but also at your life and see if any change should be made. In my case, I happen to like the particular ability that I mentioned, so I would not wish to change. At the same time, I do not want it to backfire on me, so I simply created a thoughtform (you remember those) to block any opponent from grabbing onto my blind spot and bring people to me who will warn me if such a thing is likely to occur. Also, if I am going to be in such a position where there is a great likelihood of such an occurrence, I create a thoughtform for the location I will be at and design it to block anyone who might become a problem.

How does this work? You are, I am sure, familiar with the various forms of self-protection that are used when walking in bad areas. Most people simply surround themselves with a white light, and that is often sufficient for their purposes. But sometimes someone comes along who is not receptive to that, and the individual who depends upon that simple defense is in for a shock.

I prefer something a little more aggressive. Meditate and visualize yourself as wearing a suit of armor. It does not have to be a full outfit—a simple breastplate and helmet are usually sufficient. See yourself as wearing this armor, and at the same time command that your etheric body take the form of the armor. If you can see this as being either black or red, so much the better, for in any aggressive working the more of those colors we can get, the better. Know that as you charge this image, anyone who comes near you with hostile intent will feel an overriding fear that reaches down to his very bones and he will not be able to stay in your presence. Keep working on this. It is a very effective modification of your field, so effective that I have seen large people cross the street to avoid making contact with me.

There are those who will contend that the above exercise is more in the manner of a creation of a thoughtform, but on close examination you will find there is a great difference between molding the astral or mental bodies, as you have just done, and creating a thoughtform. For one thing, the thoughtform will, after some use and charging, take on a practical life of its own. A molded field will only keep its shape as long as it is being used. Therefore, it is a good idea to remake the armor now and then until you no longer need it. If possible, keep the visualization active in the back of your mind while it is being used. This technique is not so difficult as it may seem. It is something akin to carrying on a conversation and watching a television show at the same time. There are other, more subtle, differences between a molded field and a thoughtform, but these need not concern you.

A thoughtform may also be made that will serve to strengthen and mold your field automatically, and I will cover that in another chapter. For now let us concentrate some more on your field.

I have gone on at some length about analysis, because as you progress in psionics, you will learn that most of your activity will in some way involve the ability to study your subject. Remember, the more you know about a person, the more effectively you can relate to that person. And if conflict should come, you will have a store of data that will give you a tremendous working advantage.

Up to now we have concentrated our efforts on studying the aura and the astral body. As most people are primarily influenced by their emotions, it was necessary to spend some time on the subject. But now we will take a short look at analyzing the mental level. This level is a bit harder to study because it is more complex, containing, as it were, much more information than either the aura or the astral body, but the information is somewhat harder to get at. To begin with, color plays a very small role in the mental level. There, color is simply another datum to be used or rejected. Also, much of the activity at the mental level is very transitory indeed, and thus it is very hard to grab onto a single thought and put it into the can, so to speak.

Because of these difficulties, when we study the mental level we are not going to be looking for those individual thoughts, no matter how powerful. Rather, we are going to be looking at thought patterns—how a person thinks, rather than what he thinks. In this area, psionics gives us an advantage that is not normally available.

This is not a new idea. As long as people have had conflicts, major or minor, one side has always tried to understand the other. It often takes the form of gaming, in which simulations are used to predict the possible actions of opponents from what is known about their behavior patterns. One pioneer in the area of artificial intelligence decided to have some fun back in 1964 and programmed a computer into becoming what he called the Goldwater Machine. He took the statements of then-presidential candidate Barry Goldwater and created a program that would use those statements to analyze any question put to it and come up with the answer the candidate was likely to give. The obvious flaw in this method, as everyone knows, is that what candidates for office say they will do and what they ultimately do are almost always totally different things.

So what we look for when we analyze the mental body is not what we already know about a person, but what is hidden—those patterns that do not show but are nevertheless dominant in the character of the subject. Once you know those, the mind of anyone becomes an open file.

One never studies the mental level without first making a complete analysis of the aura and the astral body. People are not dominated by thoughts but by emotions, even when they think they are being unemotional, so you must first know what the emotional nature of the subject is. Once you have that information, you may begin to look for thought patterns to emerge. In order to accomplish this, you must first look for the basic desires, likes, dislikes and other dominant features of the person's thoughts. It will thus be necessary to make a dial chart similar to the color gauge, with a pointer. When dividing the circle, make a space for each aspect of thought that is likely to influence the subject. These should include home and family, education, religious or spiritual beliefs, peer influence, work, sex, politics, health and any other you may think of. One of the nice things about these gauges is that you make new ones with great ease if the old ones become obsolete. And, as we always manage to leave something out, it is a good idea to have a space marked "other."

Once you have done this, take a rate for the mental body of the subject and set your gauge to the first place, say family. Use the stick pad to see if that is a significant determiner of the subject's thoughts. And do not be surprised if it is not. You will become amazed as you go along with this at how unimportant things can be to some people. Go around the gauge and test each category, marking on a piece of paper the ones that get a response.

After you have your list of things that influence the thoughts of your subject, get out your numerical gauge and repeat the procedure you learned to analyze colors. You want both percent and intensity. Once you have made a chart similar to the one for the colors, take a piece of paper and write "analytical" on one side and "emotional" on the other. Take the witness of the subject out of the can and place it on the paper between the words. Now get out your pendulum. I know that we have not used it much yet, but you need it now. Hold the pendulum over the witness and ask if the subject is more analytical or emotional in nature. The pendulum will swing toward the correct answer. Write that answer on the chart.

Now that you have a chart that will tell you the basic mental makeup of the subject, you can begin to study his or her thoughts. Of course, what you do with this knowledge is up to you.

Next we will look at the influence of the mental body on other people and how their mental bodies, in turn, influence us. As you can well imagine, this is a matter of some importance to anyone who works in the area of the psychic.

We must first understand that while there is no known limit to the distance the influence of the mental level may extend, that does not mean the mental body itself extends to an unknown limit. In fact, in your litle experiment measuring the size of the various bodies, you already proved that. True, the mental body is made up of the same god-stuff as every other mental body, but that does not mean that at the functional level they are the same body. Second, merely because we do not know the ultimate range of the influence of an individual mental body, that in itself does not necessarily mean that range is infinite. It is quite possible that a point can be reached somewhere out in space where telepathic transmissions from Earth can no longer be received simply because it is too far. At the present time we have absolutely no accurate way of proving such things, so it is best to assume nothing and see what kind of results future experiments bring.

Be that as it may, there is no question that the mental body and its transmissions can reach anyone anywhere on the face of the Earth. Telepathy experiments have been done involving not only people, but even animals, including very small animals, like snails. SNAILS?!

Yes, you read right, snails. In 1852, long before even I was born, a Frenchman by the name of Benoit came up with the idea that certain relationships in the animal kingdom could be proven. He must have been having dinner at the time, because he chose snails as his subjects. He gathered 52 of the little creatures, saving them from the saucepan, and set them to living in pairs. On the shell of each snail he wrote a letter, the same letter in each pair, so that one pair had two A's, another two B's, etc. Then he sent one set of lettered snails to friends in America with explicit instructions not the eat them, telling them when the experiment would take place. At the appointed day and hour, he gave a slight electric shock to snail E. It was recorded that the snail E in America became quite animated for a snail, and it was proposed that a snail telegraph be established.[2] Fortunately, nothing came of that idea, because no doubt snail lovers all over the world would have been furious.

It is easy to laugh at the great snail experiment, but on August 25, 1965, the Delawarre Laboratories conducted an experiment between Oxford and New York, using equipment somewhat more sophisticated than was available in 1852. The Delawarre people had developed a gadget called a psychoplotter, which measured changes in body tissues by the change in sound frequencies inside them, and by means of this were able to tell when subjects were responding to

---

[2] Beasley, *Your Electro-Vibratory Body*, p. 42.

their treatments. It also made a nice graph using a plotting pen and rolling paper.

Anyway, a photograph of a 17-year-old subject with a leg problem was sent to John Hay of Fairfield, Connecticut, along with a radionic treatment instrument (nice of them to include that little piece of machinery). The boy stayed in Oxford and was wired to the psychoplotter. After the plotter had been run for about an hour to determine the usual state of the leg, the boy's photograph was placed in the radionic machine at 10:20 AM EST. The graph noted a strong change. After twenty minutes, the photo was removed and the plot resumed its normal course. Another twenty minutes passed and the photo was given a shot of light from an ordinary lightbulb. Again, the plot showed a marked change.[3]

The significance of this experiment is striking, for there is no reason why it cannot be repeated in any laboratory. You can even do a similar test yourself.

You will need, in addition to a willing subject, a galvanic skin response (GSR) meter, a radionic box, and a convenient light. It is also good to have another friend to watch the subject—that way he or she can be in a different room, or even a different city, from you.

Take a rate for the subject and have him/her set the GSR meter (which can be a cheap one from a novelty or electronics store) at the point just under where either the buzzer starts or the needle moves. Have the other assistant stay by the subject to make sure that he/she does not cheat and watch the equip-

---

ment. Do not tell them when the experiment is going to begin, but do not make them wait too long, either. Not only is that impolite, it may cause your subject to get disgusted and walk out. After a few minutes, turn on the light, aiming it at the witness sample in the machine. When you do this, there should be an immediate response on the GSR meter. Have your friends note the time when this response occurred.

I know this is not going to be as good an experiment as you could conduct with more sensitive instruments, such as a polygraph, but it will give you some good, hard evidence that your radionic device is influencing the mental body of your subject, which is the level that is involved in telepathy.

Now that you have proven that the mental body exerts influence and receives it as well, you may begin to measure the degree of that influence. For this you will follow a procedure that you should be well familiar with by now.

One thing you should have learned by now is that the key to getting any answer in psionics is simply knowing the right questions to ask. In this case, you are going to take a measurement of the degree of influence a person's mental body will have on another person simply by being in the same room with him or her.

Up to now we have been taking a rate on the radionic box for the subject before asking any questions. If you feel you still need to do this, please continue, but there is a faster method which by now you should have the experience to use. For this you will need only the numerical gauge and stick pad (a plastic coffee-can lid will do quite nicely). There will be no connections made. Place the witness of the subject in front of you and ask the question as you begin to move the gauge, as you have done before. Zero means no influence whatsoever, and 100 would mean that the subject's mere presence would turn everyone into a virtual robot. The reading that you will get will be somewhere in between those.

Once you have done this with a subject, try it on yourself. Write down the figure that you get and then put on your psionic amplifying helmet and try again. You should get a reading somewhat higher than your first one. Of course, if you have a friend who can use the stick pad and gauge, so much the better. It can be very difficult to get an accurate reading when we are asking something that truly concerns us. If you have a strong interest in seeing a higher reading for something, that is what you will get. So if you must test yourself, try to be as honest and disinterested as possible, and bear in mind that there is always the possibility of self-deception. It happens to all of us. I can remember with embarrassment at least one experiment in which all of my gauges said that everything was going exactly as I planned it, when in reality the only thing that was happening was that I was fooling myself. So if you have that happen, do not let it be a bother. Simply chalk it up to experience and try to be more careful the next time. After all, it is not likely that any mistake you make with this stuff is going to blow up the house.

Never forget that the mental level is primarily concerned with thinking and is energized and expanded by mental activity, as opposed to emotional activity. It is important not to confuse the two. Fortunately, however, when experimenting, it is quite easy to eliminate the emotions entirely. There are few people who can become either ecstatic or infuriated over long addition. Of course, if you are addicted to a calculator, as I once became, it may take awhile to remember how to add at all. But this simple exercise can energize the mental body without letting emotion get in the way.

Take a reading to see just how far your mental body is reaching and what its intensity is. Write that down so you do not forget it, and then begin adding lots of numbers. Do this for about five or ten minutes and then take a new reading for your mental body. You will find that both its size and intensity are greater.

The influence of the mental body, however, is not so much in these areas. True, there are times when the presence of someone in truly deep thought will naturally cause those around him or her to become quiet, but this may be more a cultural response than any effect of the mental body. The real effectiveness lies in the fact, as I have stated before, that all telepathy comes from the mental level, though it may carry and be energized by emotional messages.

A message can only be effective when it is sent from the mental level and is clear. The greater the clarity, the greater the possibility it will influence the receiver. In *Psychic Power* we studied ways of sending clear and concise messages. Never forget that at the mental level there is almost continual activity, and any message that is sent has to get through that interference. This is why emotional messages have greater impact than purely intellectual ones, and why a thought-form, with its capacity to take root in the aura of the subject, is more effective than a directed thought.

CHAKRAS

One of the peculiarities of the etheric body is the presence, at the etheric level, of centers, or rather vortices, of energy that are called chakras. Now I know that everyone and his grand-nephew has written about these things. And if that were not bad enough, none of the writers agree on anything, except that poor Bishop Leadbeater did not know what he was talking about when he wrote his pioneering study of them, which was based *in toto* on his own clairvoyant investigations, which seem to be in conflict not only with the classical Hindu views on the subject, but with all later research, some of it quite good, done by radionic practitioners such as David Tansley.

But what all are agreed upon is that these centers are essential for the functioning of the physical body. As one lecturer put it, "You do not have to worry about opening your chakras because if they are closed you are dead." But after that, nobody agrees about anything. First, no one is quite sure just how many there are. They try to keep the number of the major ones at seven, because of both tradition and the idea that each chakra has one of the seven colors attached to it, causing more confusion. But then they add minor chakras and fight over which are major and which are minor.

51

For example, David Tansley, who has done what is probably the best research in this area, is convinced that the spleen chakra, while essential, is a minor chakra, and thus has room for the pelvic chakra while keeping to the sacred seven. There is a small problem with this, for we can be sure of the function of the spleen chakra, and that function is to make sure that the body gets its proper dose of prana, or vital energy, the stuff which keeps it running. How he can say the chakra that performs that most necessary of functions is a minor one is beyond me. At least Dr. Tansley does not go to the ridiculous extreme of some others who ascribe to each chakra a certain function and then try to carry that function out in the way societies act. We have to be careful when making judgments about these things, so please take everything I say here with a bit of salt and remember that we are in an area where there is much disagreement. Like our study of the field, you must be willing to experiment for yourself to see what works and what is true.

I differ from most of the students of this subject in that I use an eight-chakra system. This includes the seven traditional chakras and the pelvic chakra, which controls the reproductive system. In this I have taken the Tansley interpretation and restored the spleen to its place of honor.

Much of what has been written about chakras concerns the use of these vortices as means of gaining psychic abilities. At one time this was of great importance, as there was no other way, besides ritual, of increasing these talents. With the aid of psionic devices, however, that need is largely gone, and the fact is that increasing the activity of a particular chakra at the expense of the others can create more problems than it is worth. Therefore, I will not waste your time with meditations on each chakra. You simply do not need them. For those actions that require the use of a specific chakra, you will find that you probably have, assuming that you are in reasonable physical and mental health, more than enough energy available now.

The purpose of our studying the chakras is not so much how they can be used as how they can be controlled. One of the few times that the dire warnings of the older writers makes sense is when they talk about the problems that can come from chakras working too hard, too soon. This is usually associated with the phenomenon known as kundalini, the rise of energy in the etheric body up the spinal column into the brain. This is an energy that usually lies dormant in all of us, and it may be best that it stays that way.

It is very easy to laugh at the cautions given by such authors as Bishop Leadbeater on this subject. Much of his concern was grounded in Victorian moralizing. But in the case of kundalini, the Bishop was right. There are very real, practical problems that can result from letting this force run rampant through your etheric body.

First, you must understand that each chakra functions in such a way as to affect certain organs and functions of the physical body. If a chakra gets out of control, that organ or function can be damaged, sometimes quite seriously. I know of no case where it has actually killed someone, but it can make a person very uncomfortable and very sick.

Second, and this is perhaps more important, is

the possibility of psychological damage. There are certain psychic abilities that do come from the rise of the kundalini energy, but if these are unexpected, or worse, uncontrolled, they can make it impossible for an individual to live any sort of normal life. There are few instances more tragic than the person who suddenly finds that he or she can see the astral plane and then discovers, with horror, that he/she can no longer distinguish between the astral and physical worlds!

Leave kundalini alone!

So much for the dire warnings. Now back to the chakras.

As I said, I have found that an eight-chakra system is best for my work. As you progress in your own experience, you may wish to use a different one, but in this book, the eight-chakra system is the one I use.

It is traditional in discussing each chakra that we start from the bottom and work up, kind of like climbing a totem pole (and please do not take that literally). There are no major chakras in the legs, so the first one that we encounter is, appropriately enough, the base chakra. This is also sometimes called the anal or sacral chakra, though the term "sacral" is also sometimes applied to the pelvic chakra. You see how confusing this can get. Anyway, the base chakra is roughly located at the bottom of the spine, but you probably knew or guessed that already. This chakra is primarily concerned with the spine itself. It is also the place where kundalini is supposed to be stored, laying coiled up and waiting to burst forth. Because of its relationship with the spine, the lower parts of the nervous system are controlled by the action of this chakra.

Next we encounter the pelvic chakra. The location

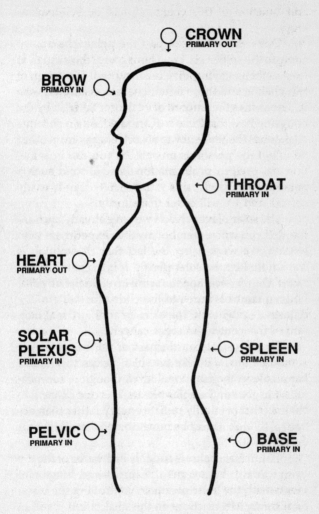

Figure 3 - The Chakras

and function of this chakra should be self-explanatory.

Once we have risen past the pelvic chakra, we come to the spleen chakra. This is one of the biggies, at least as far as staying alive is concerned. The action of this chakra, and those minor chakras associated with it, determines the amount of vital force taken in by the body and how that force is distributed. As a result, this chakra has the tendency to absorb energy from other people if the person is unwell. As you can imagine, this can present problems for those around such a person. Fortunately, this is a difficulty that is easily solved, and we will cover that shortly.

The solar plexus chakra we have already encountered. If you will remember my little experiment with hunger, we were using the fact that all emotion is transmitted by the solar plexus. It is a direct link between the physical and the astral level. In the physical body, it controls much of the endocrine system, the digestive system and the skin. In addition, malfunction of this center can cause cancer.

The physical counterpart of the heart chakra should be obvious. Like the solar plexus, this chakra has a role in the emotional level, though not as profound as that of the solar plexus. It is one of the two chakras that primarily radiate energy rather than absorb it, though it must be remembered that all chakras do both.

The throat chakra is roughly in the area of the top of the throat. It governs the throat and lungs and works with the solar plexus in controlling the intestinal tracts. Malfunctions in this chakra can result in such things as allergies, fatigue, menstrual irregularities and asthma, as well as all diseases of the throat and its glands.

The two brain chakras, the brow and the crown chakras, are a bit difficult to pin down as to their physical manifestations. The brow chakra is generally assumed to control the pituitary gland, which is the dominant gland in the endocrine system, and is assumed to be responsible for growth. More importantly, for our purposes, the brow chakra is a major psychic receptor point. It is the location of the "third eye," and all psychic transmissions that are first handled by the mental body come through here first.

The crown chakra seems to be the controlling center for the entire system. It is related to the pineal gland, and all functions of that gland are controlled by this chakra. The crown chakra is the other main emitter of energy in the chakra system. In this way it cooperates with the brow chakra, which controls the eyes as receivers of psychic energy, while the crown controls them when they function as emitters.

As I said earlier, we will start by learning the procedures for controlling the functions of the chakras. They are really quite simple and should present you with little trouble.

The malfunction of any one chakra can produce various side effects in the physical body. Therefore, by knowing how to restore a chakra to normal, balanced operation, you will be able to improve your health. At this point I will repeat my warnings from my last book. *Do not, under any circumstances, take any money for using a psionic method to help anyone, particularly in matters of health.* You can get into terrible legal trouble if you do. Also, never consider psionics as a substitute for conventional medicine. Rather, use it as a supplement and keep it secret. Even if your machines indicate that you or someone else is cured, do not stop conventional treatment until the diagnosis is confirmed by standard means. There are too many idiots dying because they prefer the nonsense of faith healers and witch doctors as it is. Do not be one of them.

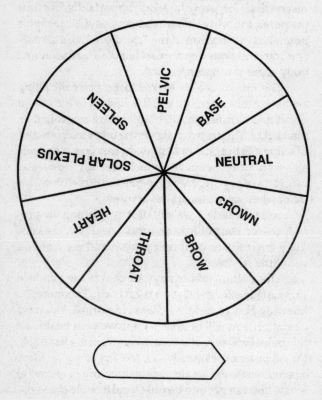

Figure 4

Now that we have that out of the way, here is how you work with chakras. You will have to make another gauge. In fact, you may want to make two. The first one will look something like Figure 4. You will notice that I have left a space for a neutral position. This is to make asking an all-important question easier; namely, is the particular problem caused by the malfunction of a particular chakra?

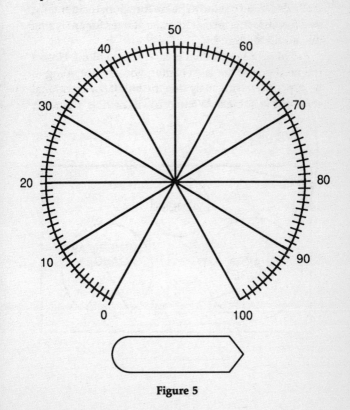

Figure 5

Once you have made the circle for the chakra gauge, make another numerical gauge that will look like Figure 5. Before you attach the pointers, cut out your gauges and glue them to a sheet of cardboard. Make a small circle between them for the witness sample, and you should have a sheet that looks like Figure 6. Once you have done this, you may make and attach your pointers. You now have a double gauge specifically designed to study chakra function. Incidentally, you may use this format to make gauges for analyzing just about anything.

This is a system that is rarely done blind. Unlike the methods of the last chapter, you are not going to be concerned with analyzing the mental or emotional state of the subject. What you will have is a person,

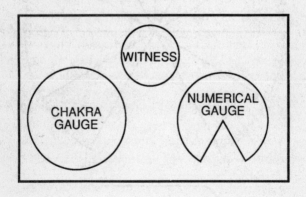

Figure 6

probably a friend or family member, who is not feeling very well, and in fact, may be in death's waiting room. Hence you may already know what is wrong and will use that information to aid you in using the chakras to help the person.

Let us say that your Aunt Mathilda is in the hospital. She is doing quite poorly and you think that you might like to be of some help to her. You are already using the general balancing method taught you in *Psychic Power*, but this is having little effect. Therefore you decide to use the chakras to improve her health.

First you must find out if the illness is related to an imbalance in a specific chakra. In spite of much that has been written, most externally caused diseases, which are the result of strange bugs and viruses, are not related to chakra function. So there is little point in using the chakras to help them.

Set up your chakra analyzing gauge that you have just made and place the witness in the place provided. Once you have done this, set the chakra dial to neutral and the disruption (numerical) dial to zero. Ask the stick pad if treating a chakra will help the condition of your aunt. If you get a stick, continue; if not, the problem is probably not chakra-oriented, and working with them will be a waste of time. You may also use a pendulum to answer the above question.

Assuming that you get a positive response from either the pad or the pendulum, you must then determine which chakra is in most need of treatment. Set the chakra dial at the "base" segment and stroke the pad, mentally asking if this is the one to work on. If you get a stick, stop there and ask the numerical dial what level of disruption is present. By now you should have enough experience with the numerical gauge, so this should be no problem. The purpose of taking a numerical reading is to discover not only how bad the situation is but also how the subject is progressing.

Once you have a reading for the level of disruption, write it down, because this operation is going to take some time, depending on how serious the situation is.

Now that you know that Aunt Mathilda has something worse than the cold everyone thought she had (at least until she entered the hospital), you have to determine the method of treatment. This means that you will need your radionic box, your pendulum, and some colored gels, usually available at camera shops. It is also a good idea to have a small lamp available.

The first thing that you will do is find the treatment rate for the particular chakra. You do this by writing the name of the chakra, in this case the "base" chakra, on a small piece of paper. There is an even better method of doing this, but that will have to wait for the chapter on patterns, so turn to that if you wish to learn it immediately. For our purposes now, simply writing down which chakra we are treating will be sufficient. Place this piece of paper in the can with the witness of your aunt and take a rate. This rate will correspond with the disruption of the chakra. After this is done, balance the rate as you learned to do in *Psychic Power*.

You will remember that in the previous chapter I gave you an experiment using light to energize a witness sample to prove the fact that people can be influenced at a distance. Now we will use a similar principle for healing. Take the witness of Aunt Mathilda out of the can and place it on the stick pad of the machine. This will put her on the receiving end of the circuit.

Lay the colored gels in a semicircle on the table in front of you. It is a good idea to get the seven basic colors of the spectrum, in which case you could use the color gauge and stick pad instead of the pendulum, but it is only necessary to have the three primary colors—red, blue and yellow. Either way, ask which color is best to treat the condition of this chakra. Once you have this information, lay the colored gel on top of the witness sample and turn on the lamp so that the gel is directly in the beam. In this way the wavelengths of the colored light will act on the witness sample and thence will be transmitted to the subject. Some practitioners ask their pendulums to tell them how long each treatment should last, but I have found from experience that a standard treatment time of two hours a night is about right for most people. Remember, the room light will also filter through the gel, so the lamp is merely adding a little extra boost. In any event, it is not good to be dogmatic about this stuff. Experiment and find out what works best for you.

While this is going on, your aunt's doctor will be calling in various specialists and Uncle Harry will be planning the funeral, and you can experience the shocked looks on their faces when your aunt begins to recover. Just be certain not to mention what you have done. Some doctors have actually heard of radionics and they tend to become quite animated about it, and as we do not wish to cause anyone to have a heart attack or a stroke, it is best not to say anything.

This is the basic procedure for treating and controlling the activity of any given chakra. Leave the rate for about a week before testing again, to find out if there has been any change in the degree of disruption. Assuming that there has been, take a new rate and balance it and re-ask the pendulum or gauge which color to transmit. Keep this up until the chakra is at zero disruption. Once that point has been reached, you may return to treating the physical part, such as heart or lungs, etc.

You can see that with this ability provided by psionics, there is no need for the elaborate and often dangerous meditations prescribed for activating the various chakras. Also, you have the ability to correct for any problems that may arise from working in this area. One cannot stress too strongly the fact that the greater the psychic ability, the greater the need for control. Now that you know how that control is exercised, you can begin to learn how to efficiently use the chakras for psychic purposes.

You will remember that I stressed in my short overview of the centers that while each chakra acts as both an emitter and a receiver of energy, some are primarily receivers, while others are primarily emitters. This is very important to working with the chakras, because those who try to use a chakra and its energy in the wrong way often fail, if they are lucky.

You will not be using the base chakra for any psychic work unless you wish someone to get a bad case of premature kundalini, so let's begin with the pelvic chakra. This chakra controls the physical genitals and by extension the sexual drives of the person. It is primarily a receiver of energy, and its use should be obvious. When transmitting to this center, you must be careful to transmit only physical responses. It will not respond to a verbal command, or even to an emotion. It is, therefore, a very difficult target without the benefit of psionics. There is only one way to work on it.

You will need a witness of the subject, a radionic box set up to take a plug from your psionic amplifying helmet, the helmet and the connecting wire, and a piece of paper with "pelvic chakra" written on it. Set up the machine and helmet for a contact rate that will direct your thoughts to the subject's pelvic chakra. This is done by placing both the witness and the paper in the can and taking a rate on both the box and the helmet. Now all you have to do is put on the helmet and do whatever is necessary to get yourself extremely sensually excited.

Moving up the line, we have the spleen chakra to deal with. Because of its peculiar role in controlling the distribution of prana, or vital energy, to the physical body, most of your work with this chakra will be therapeutic. Not only can you increase the amount of vital energy in your subject, but you can help yourself as well.

Once in a while you may come across the term "psychic vampire." This is a person who, consciously or unconsciously, drains energy from another person. They are usually quite inconsiderate and refuse to either wear a black cape or speak with an eastern European accent while doing it. You can always tell if you are around such a person because you will feel quite drained after only a few minutes. And that is what is happening, you are quite literally being drained. So what do you do? You can hardly attack the person with a wooden stake, and waving garlic may only cause the person to run for the nearest cookbook. There is no need for such foolishness. You can protect yourself by means of a simple visualization.

When you meditate, concentrate on your own spleen chakra. Now create a thoughtform in the form of a valve, which can be nothing more than a tube with a hinged flap. Visualize this flap as opening and closing towards you, so that when you inhale it is open and when you exhale, the force of energy going out pushes it shut. Hold this image in your mind and then command it to be activated whenever you are around the person. Thus the flow of vital energy will come into your system as usual, but whenever the person you are guarding against is near, the valve will block any outflow from your spleen chakra. You should notice two things. First, you will feel much better, and second, the person will not bother you so much.

You may also use the spleen chakra to give a much-needed boost to the vital energy of a person who is very sick. But you have to do it right or you can get into trouble.

Let us assume that your Aunt Mathilda is in the hospital again, and this time she is in a very bad way indeed. There is no time to use the normal balancing or energizing methods. She needs a good, strong shot of vital energy and she needs it now.

Take the witness of Aunt Mathilda and place it in the radionic box with the paper that says "spleen chakra." Take a contact rate. Using the numerical chart, ask first what level of energy is necessary to keep Aunt Mathilda alive. Once you have this, ask what level she is at now. This will give an idea of how well you are doing. All you have to do now is shine a red light on the witness of Aunt Mathilda. There will be an immediate improvement in her condition as the red energy is sent to her spleen chakra.

Now for a couple words of warning. Everyone dies eventually, and even psionics can, at best, put off the inevitable for only a while. It may be that Aunt Mathilda is so far gone that the kindest thing is to let her die in peace.

Another thing to beware of is acting foolishly. There are certain emergency-type situations where the first reaction a knowledgeable person does is to, by simple visualization, transfer vital energy from him/herself to the sick person. This is not a good thing to do. No matter how young or healthy or strong you are, you cannot afford to give up one iota of your own vital energy. The entire balance of your own body's functioning is based on there being a steady flow of that energy, and if you start giving it away, you will pay dearly in the very near future, like when the next flu epidemic strikes.

I know that this chapter is beginning to sound like a collection of don'ts, but please bear with me. There are a lot of things that can go wrong if the chakras and their energy are not treated with some respect, and I would not want you to encounter a disaster because I failed to warn you about it.

With that we can leave the spleen chakra and move on. We have dealt with the solar plexus chakra already in the previous chapter. Simply remember that when you transmit to this chakra, you can only transmit emotion, not a physical response or an intellectual concept. The solar plexus center is only open to feeling.

This brings us to the heart chakra. The heart chakra is the principal emitter of emotional energy, but there is some question about the nature of the energy that it transmits best. There are those who contend that all forms of emotion come shooting out of this center with equal force, while others will contend that only emotions of affection and love will work. I must confess that I am not sure myself. Clearly all emotions can be transmitted, and usually anger is the one that transmits the best. By the same token, anger is not healthy for the physical heart and therefore may not be a good thing to send out from this chakra. I can only suggest that you do some experiments of your own to find out how your system reacts. Certainly, the heart chakra responds best to affection.

The throat chakra is associated with not only the functions that I have already mentioned in my overview but also much of the sensory responses of the brain. This is why instructions to transmit to the back of the neck are so effective. Any input to this chakra automatically activates the involuntary nervous system, and thus if the command to "turn" is sent, the chakra sends the message to the involuntary system and the subject turns without thinking, while a purely sensory image, such as my now infamous drill, will bring an even more pronounced response. It is even possible to send a more intellectual verbal message to this center, but it is best to confine such transmissions to the brow chakras.

The brow chakra is one of the two head chakras, and both it and the crown chakra cooperate in the practice of psychic power. The brow acts as the receiver and the crown as the transmitter. Both are wired to the eyes, and thus if a thought is sent to the eyes, it is seen being shifted to the brow chakra, while if it is transmitted, the energy comes out of the crown chakra, as I will explain shortly.

Any thought can be transmitted to the brow chakra. This is the center that you will aim at when you send a command or an idea to a target subject. This can be done by one of two methods. The first is simple visualization.

Let us assume that your Uncle Harry is so happy about Aunt Mathilda's miraculous recoveries that he has taken to humming Sousa marches during football games. He does not hum very well, and your aunt is beginning to wish that he had his twitch back. At least it kept him occupied. This would not be a problem for you, except that it is Thanksgiving and he is trying to hum with a mouthful of sage dressing. Not only is this being very disrespectful to the memory of your great-great grandmother, who originated the recipe, but it is disgusting as well. You are trying to send him a psychic message to be quiet and swallow his food, but you cannot get through to him. If this is the case, you have to aim directly for the brow chakra.

Visualize a cross, like the astrological symbol for Earth, right on the center of the forehead. Now aim the beam from your eyes at that point and send the message to "be quiet!" as strongly as you can. Uncle Harry should give a little start and swallow automatically.

If your subject is at a distance, you may direct your sending to that point with the aid of your machine and helmet. It is not necessary to set up the contact rate to the brow chakra of the subject, though you may if you wish. The normal contact rate to the subject should be sufficient. Of course, when using the tele-flasher, the more specific the aim, the better, but we are not using it at this point.

Once you have the contact rate for the subject on both box and helmet, you should have little trouble holding the image of the subject in your mind. Once you have that image, try to concentrate on the brow chakra to the exclusion of the rest of the face. This is not really as difficult as it sounds. With practice in visualization, and you should have a lot of that by now, you will discover that you can zero in on any part of the image at will.

While holding the image of the brow chakra in your mind, think the message that you are going to send. In the case of the brow chakra, you can send ver-bal messages with no trouble, as this is the center that is designed to receive them. I have found it useful to use the counting string for these, with each knot being pulled through the fingers as the message is repeated. If you have one already, this is simply a string of 25 knots tied along it. It can be quite helpful because even with a psionic amplifying helmet, you may have trou-ble holding an image. By running the string, each time you feel a knot, if you are losing the image, you can rebuild it before thinking the message and thus your sendings become more powerful. A subject who is on the receiving end of this technique is, quite literally, a sitting duck. It is almost impossible for him or her not to receive what you are sending.

There is one more use for the brow chakra that I have never really needed, though it is fun to experi-ment with, and that is the capacity to visualize very small things, such as atoms. This is done by imagining a very small tube, like a fiber optic, coming out of the brow chakra and focusing on the object to be studied. Around the turn of the century, Annie Besant and Bishop Leadbeater did a series of investigations of minerals this way and published their findings in a book entitled *Occult Chemistry*. No one took their studies very seriously until a few years ago, when a physicist named Stephen Phillips noticed a remarkable similarity between their drawings and the cloud atoms. He dug further and his conclusion can be restated by the phrase "My God! They were right!" So you may want to try something similar for yourself.[4]

Now we can move on to the crown chakra. This is the principle emitter of all psychic energy, both coming out of the chakra itself and the eyes. In Figure 7 you can see how this energy works. Path *A* takes the energy from the crown chakra through the optic nerves to the eyes, while the energy emitted directly from the chakra follows the lines of the etheric body (*B*) down to the beam coming from the eyes and links up with it. This is why the eyes have traditionally been considered the most powerful transmission points for this energy.

One of the features of the crown chakra is that it emits such a powerful blast of energy when being used that when this energy is forced downward into the brain area, it can actually hurt. This is why, unlike most radionic devices that do not need an antenna, the psionic amplifying helmet has to have one, to act

---

[4] Dr. Phillips' book, *The ESP of Quarks*, is, unfortunately, almost unreadable unless you have an advanced degree in physics. His article "Extrasensory Perception of Subatomic Particles" (*Fate*, April, May 1987) explains things in a much more understandable fashion.

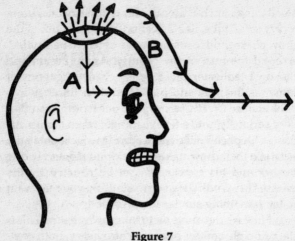

Figure 7

as a wave guide directing the main flow of the chakra energy outward, even when the helmet is used in a receiver mode.

At this point you may be wondering why the plate in the helmet is kept on the crown chakra instead of having a second plate for the brow. I found that a forehead plate was quite uncomfortable at all times, so I was forced to rely on the crown plate. I assume that it receives as well as it transmits because of the fact that all chakras work both ways. The difference is in the level of power used for either input or emission.

The crown chakra works automatically. It is neither necessary nor desirable for you to visualize thought energy being poured out of the chakra. To do so will only increase the activity of that chakra to possibly dangerous levels. Let it work on its own and you will have no trouble with it.

THOUGHTFORMS

In my last book, and in this one as well, I have made frequent references to thoughtforms, and in *Psychic Power*, I taught you the basics of their manufacture and use. Now it is time to go into a little (well, actually quite a lot) more detail as to how they are made, how they work and how you can use them to make life more enjoyable and meaningful.

In many ways, even more than psionic devices, the thoughtform is the basic tool of psychic function. It is the means by which our thoughts are made more powerful and therefore more effective. Because of this fact, the better you are able to create and use thoughtforms, the more effective you will be.

Let's look at the thoughtform itself and begin to understand a bit how it works.

A thoughtform is a clump of very basic psychic energy. It may even be considered to be a form of pre-matter. It contains information, and this information determines how its energy will function. Once it is created and set to work, the more coherent it is, the more likely it will be to influence events in the physical world. This influence takes the form of what can be considered psychokinesis, but a psychokinesis of a type that creates coincidence. For this reason, we will term the action IPK, for incidental psychokinesis, as opposed to the sort of thing that occurs when a psychic tries to move objects by direct will.

Got that? The thoughtform is made up of those particles that I posited earlier, the psions. Each psion has polarity, and thus positive and negative psions attract, just as positive and negative poles of a magnet do. It is therefore impossible to have a thoughtform with less than two particles, and the number of particles in any given thoughtform will always be even. At least that is the hypothesis we are working on. If there is an odd number of psions, the basic coherence of the thoughtform will be upset and the thoughtform will dissipate.

In this model the production of the thoughtform works something like this. When the mental level sends a message to the physical brain, the waveform involved causes the appropriate neurons to fire. As this occurs, the fact that life energy is involved causes a new wave to be sent outward from the physical body to the level appropriate to the nature of the thought. At this point it is still a wave. But along the way something happens. The psychic stuff that makes up the various energy fields of our bodies interferes with the wave and causes it to kind of scrunch together.

Let me use an analogy. It is a foggy morning and the freeway is crowded with cars, all moving at a pretty good clip, rather close together, and seen from the air they make a continuously moving line. All of a sudden the lead driver of this line runs into a patch of very heavy fog and slams on his brakes. The other cars are moving too fast to stop quickly and are too close together to miss each other, and very soon, amid much crunching of metal and breaking of glass, twenty cars are packed into a space that would normally hold three, and from the air it looks as if something terrible has happened in an accordion factory.

This is what happens to the wave. It gets jammed together and the result is the formation of a basic particle, perhaps *the* basic particle—the psion.

Each time the wave hits an interference pattern, it forms at least one psion, and any given thought will produce a bunch of them, the amount determined by the intensity of the thought and the length of time the thought is held.

So you have a bunch of these little psions floating around in space, each containing the information from the thought and each having polarity. What happens then?

The psions will naturally attract each other and, in doing so, acquire mass. Very small mass, to be sure, but mass nonetheless. This means that the thoughtform thus created cannot stay at the purely mental level. It is either propelled through the void to a specific target, moves back towards the person and takes root in either the astral level or the aura (depending upon the mass of the thoughtform), or it joins with a massive, preexisting thoughtform that sits like an amorphous blob floating in the general mental atmosphere or forms a tight, very coherent and potentially very powerful thoughtform within the already existing large one.

A thoughtform cannot remain at the mental level of an individual. This is important because you will often find earlier writers speaking of their clairvoyant findings of thoughtforms in the mental body. Upon closer examination, however, you will discover that what they are really looking at is the astral level and merely getting their information confused. A thought-form is like a cannon shot. Given enough force, it can fly to a target or it can fall to Earth, but it will not float in the air. It is just a bit too heavy to do that.

Most thoughtforms are neither very powerful nor coherent. As a result, they do not hold together very well and do not last very long. If you can imagine each thoughtform as a light, you will notice that around any given person you will see lots of small lights flicking on and off, like Christmas tree bulbs. A few stay on rather longer, growing gradually dimmer until they too disappear, and a very few continue to burn with a consistent brightness. This is the normal state of affairs.

A problem with working on thoughtforms comes when you run across the traditional belief that the more people concentrating on a single thing, the more likely that thing will come about. I hate to disappoint anyone, but that is very rarely true. The fact of the matter is that in thoughtforms, as in dinner, too many cooks spoil the broth. There is a way around this problem that I will explain later in this chapter.

Why should this be? The power of a thoughtform to influence events (IPK) depends not so much on the amount of energy in the thoughtforms as it does on the coherency of the thought itself. Each thoughtform created by an individual has at least two psions, each containing information directly relating to the thought but also containing sidebands of stray images and emotions that the given thought will evoke. Each sideband will decrease the coherence of the thoughtform.

In fact, by now you will have noticed that one of the greatest problems that you face with your own visualization work, which includes thoughtform creation, is the tendency of the mind to just take off on its own without your knowing about it until it is too late to bring it back. If you are having this kind of trouble, just think of the problems other people who are working on a group visualization must have trying to hold onto their thoughts, and you have been working on rather concrete images.

We can, for our purposes, calculate the number of psions in any given thoughtform as $2+X$. X will always be unknown, but this gives us a point at which to start. As each psion will have at least one sideband, the formula for the coherence of any thoughtform will be $1/2+X$. Now let us figure in the number of people trying to put energy into the thoughtform. This will give us the following formula for the coherence of any given thoughtform: $C=1/(2+X)P$, where P is the number of individuals working on the thoughtform. (Not bad for someone who flunked algebra in high school, is it?) We will term this the Principle of Ultimate Instability. What that means is no thoughtform is going to last forever, and the ability of the thoughtform to actually influence people and events will be in inverse proportion to the number of people trying to work on it. This is particularly true of those attempts by various groups who try to get large numbers of people to concentrate on one thing, but it can also cause strange things to happen to small groups when they try to create a thoughtform.

Let me tell you another story. One time I got very upset with the people in our study center because they consistently refused to believe that mere thoughts could influence their physical reality. So I figured that I would show them and set up a little experiment. We all sat in a circle and tried to visualize a blue sphere over a piece of paper in the center of the circle. You must understand that the mix of people in the group virtually guaranteed that the form created would be extremely unstable, and as I had them aiming for a specific target, would be very powerful. In fact, I was beginning to worry that it might be just a bit too powerful. We were meeting in the library of the Theosophical Society headquarters in Wheaton, Illinois, and there are a few objects of some value in that building. I started to worry that one of them might break, for there was no way to predict how the unstable energy of the thoughtform would release itself. Fortunately that did not happen. But what did happen was painful enough, for just as some of the members began to actually see the sphere, an electric shock went around the circle, causing all of us to jump, in order. That ended the experiment.

But as you can see, coherence is the main concern. With an abstract principle, such as peace, coherence is almost impossible, and the well-meaning folk who gather to try to meditate on bringing peace to the world are wasting their time. The truth of the matter is that while they are feeding a blob of energy that can influence nothing, one adolescent playing a videogame on his computer can create a thoughtform for war that will be much more effective. There is a way around this problem and I will come to it later.

In spite of what I have just said, even the most incoherent thoughtform will contain a tremendous amount of energy, simply because it remains as a thoughtform, but this energy will be more in the form of potential energy rather than kinetic energy. It will not be able to influence events in and of itself, but it can be tapped and used by individuals. We find this situation no more obvious than that in religions.

I am not going to get drawn into a debate over the existence or nature of the divine. That is not the purpose of what I am now going to explain, so do not get these ideas confused. Great Jehovah may, in fact, exist somewhere, but whether or not He does is irrelevant to the fact that a very large and very incoherent thoughtform corresponding to Him does. As annoying as this may be to the religious beliefs of some, this is a truth that we will deal with. There is no possible way that the prayers and thoughts of millions over a period of centuries cannot create a thoughtform, and the Principle of Ultimate Instability requires that that thoughtform be very incoherent. In fact, the thoughtform that corresponds to the Christian deity may be visualized as a cloud with an elderly male face floating around on its surface.

These religious thoughtforms may be tapped into by a number of different methods, some of them traditional, some of them magickal, some of them psionic. The magickal technique is outside of the purview of this book, and we will cover the psionic technique in detail in the next chapter. It is the traditional method that concerns us in this chapter.

Much as one with my liberal Protestant upbringing hates to admit it, the Roman Catholic thoughtform of the Virgin Mary is one of the most powerful and coherent of the religious thoughtforms. It is matched only by certain cultic (in the nonpejorative sense) deities in India. And the reason for this is obvious. Here you have a cult dedicated to the worship of a specific individual with a definite character and history, who has well-defined physical characteristics that have become part of the tradition. Combine this with a ritual specific to that being, and you have worshippers working on a very well-defined image and idea. In short, just what you need for a good, coherent thoughtform. As a result, while the Principle of Ultimate Instability still applies, it is somewhat blunted and some very interesting and at times bizarre things can occur. These are usually the result of a spontaneous tapping of the thoughtform, combined with a variety of religious poltergeist activity.

What do I mean by this? For an excellent example, we must go to Portugal to a place called Fatima.

As I said, I was raised liberal Protestant, and to say that my opinion of the cult of Mary was not very pious would be an understatement indeed. Never was this more true of me than when I was a good, materialistic adolescent. So one Good Friday afternoon I was looking for something to do, and I turned on my television and discovered what is undoubtedly one of the most unintentionally hilarious movies ever made: *The Miracle of Our Lady of Fatima*.

The first time I saw it, I laughed so hard that I almost fell out of my chair. The story line is sappy and the acting is atrocious. Combine that with the idea of a strange woman appearing in treetops and, well, you get the message. And to make matters worse, it claimed to be a portrayal of real events. These events included the Sun doing a dance and mud being instantly dried, along with the usual quota of healings that are required in such stories.

Now if this had happened in, say, 252 A.D., we could put it down to some strange drug that got mixed in with the sacramental wine, but this was 1917, in living memory, particularly in the early 1950s when the film was made. Therefore I actually managed to put my laughter and my prejudices aside and wonder if part of the story was true. So I did a little investigating over the years and found that much of the events were as shown, with allowance for some dreadful dramatic license. Three children did see some strange woman floating in the treetops, and these visions attracted a crowd on a day that culminated in thousands (just how many is not really known; no one was counting heads) of people seeing the Sun act very strangely; and the ground, which had been a muddy mess from a driving rain, dried. There were also several prophecies given, in the usual vein of such events, and the third of these is still secret, thus leading to much speculation, which probably helps to keep interest in the whole thing alive.

But we are concerned with that final day, when the Sun danced and the ground dried. For what happened that day is unquestionably a thoughtform that went berserk.

Let us begin by examining the physical phenomena. There is no question that the ground was mud and then dried by the heat of the jumping Sun. There are too many witnesses to doubt that. There is also no question that the Sun was seen to move towards the Earth. This image was recorded by people living almost forty miles away. It is also true that at no time in

1917 did the relative positions of the Earth and Sun change. So it must be assumed that what was seen at Fatima was an optical illusion, but one of such power that it was seen for some distance.

Now let us examine the participants. The three children are of peasant stock, uneducated, living in a society that has officially disavowed religion. We have seen the pattern too many times in history to mistake it. The eldest child, a girl, is approaching puberty, and there is no question that she was the prime recipient of the visions and prophecies. The other two children are much younger and by all accounts received the visions in a more or less secondary role. The crowds see nothing but the Sun and the mud.

The fact that the eldest girl, Lucia, is approaching puberty seems here to be the key, for that is the age when poltergeist phenomena are most likely to erupt. You may well wonder why I am bringing the nature of the poltergeist into this discussion. It is because I am convinced that the key to Fatima lies in such activity.

The poltergeist is, as we know, a mind on the rampage, as one author once put it. The faculty that produces true psychokinesis, which lies dormant in us all, is activated by a process we know virtually nothing of, and it manifests in various unpredictable and usually destructive ways. While the events at Fatima were on a massive scale, they were nothing more than the poltergeist grown large, as would be expected from a mind energized by both a thought-form and the directed energy of a huge crowd.

Figure 8 gives you an idea of what probably occurred. Lucia is given a shot of power from the basic thoughtform, #1. From this and her own natural psychic

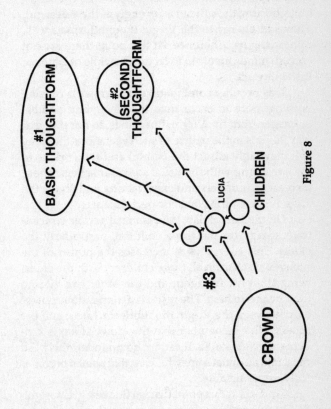

Figure 8

capacity, she creates a second thoughtform, #2. This thoughtform takes the form of the Virgin and is coherent enough to actually become visible to the two other children, who have also tapped into the larger thoughtform, though not as strongly as the eldest girl. They add energy to the Virgin thoughtform as well, reinforcing its coherence. At this point there are not enough minds involved to let the Principle of Ultimate Instability act.

This peculiar combination of energies is causing nothing more to occur than the vision and audible messages from the Virgin. But things do not stay that way, for it is in the nature of such visitations that they will inevitably attract the faithful and the curious to the site, along with the usual souvenir sellers. These increase in numbers and expectations, and finally the stage is set for the climactic performance.

On the fateful day, thousands of people concentrate energy on the three children, particularly the eldest. This energy (#3) increases the power of the transmissions from all three children, with the eldest being the primary agent and the other two adding their beams to hers. The result is a tremendous power loop between the Virgin thoughtform, Lucia, and the others. Now remember that this power loop is fundamentally unstable. It cannot go on indefinitely but must find an outlet somewhere. At that point it becomes truly unpredictable.

And it is at this point that we find our greatest difficulty. For while we know (or at least think we know) how the energies involved in the Fatima miracle worked, we do not know why they took the particular form they did. In that regard, we are faced with the classical problem involved in all poltergeist manifestations. The mind of the primary operator unconsciously instructs the energy and then it goes to work. What was floating around in the subconscious of Lucia at that point we cannot begin to guess at.

Anyway, that is essentially what happened at Fatima. Once the principal miracle occurs, however, the Principle of Ultimate Instability takes over, and thus the Virgin disappears for all practical purposes. That thoughtform is replaced by a far more unstable one which has, however, a much greater pool of energy to draw upon, and which can be tapped into at a later time by the faithful. We find something much similar at Lourdes, and we will learn how to tap that energy in the next chapter.

So much for the big stuff. I do not expect you to make anything quite that powerful, and I doubt that you would want to. They can be much more trouble than they are worth. Most of the stuff you will work with will be very small, very coherent and very powerful. In *Psychic Power* you learned how to make a basic thoughtform, so now you can go to work and learn to make thoughtforms that will be even more effective.

Much of what we will now cover may seem like a complicated rehash of the basic material in *Psychic Power*, but bear with me and study it. The time will come when you will want not only to create very powerful thoughtforms but also to analyze those of others.

There are three inherent characteristics of a functional thoughtform. These are form, function and identity. It is possible to create a very short-term thoughtform that will simply have form and function; the ones I instructed you about in *Psychic Power* were of that type. But for any thoughtform that is going to last, you must give it a name. This is not so much important to the thoughtform, which will have a very limited intelligence at best, but to yourself, because it makes calling up the power or function of that thoughtform so much easier.

Let us begin with form. The purpose of a thoughtform may be embodied in its shape, for we know that certain shapes seem to have an intrinsic meaning. For example, a shield is always defensive, even if it seems to be used in an aggressive role. A sword, having two edges, can be seen as either aggressive or defensive in its nature, but always combative. A spear and its modern variant, the rocket, is always aggressive. Let us use the four traditional symbols of magick: the rod, the cup, the shield or disk, and the sword to explain how these can be used.

The rod can be seen as a connecting link, such as telephone wires, which are really nothing but very long rods stretched out over great distances. All beams are rods. Therefore, anytime you make a thoughtform in the shape of a rod, you would be making a connection of some kind.

The cup, on the other hand, is always a receptacle. A cup holds things; things are placed or poured into it. Energy can be poured into a cup and stored there for later use. The energy can be made to flow along a rod into a cup.

I have already covered the shield and sword, and they can be used in combination. The sword also has the capacity to divide, a useful tool when facing a combination of hostile people or forces.

Most objects fall under these four headings. A lightbulb can be grouped with the rod. Why? Because the light that comes out of it connects the bulb with whatever the light falls upon. The mirror can be considered a shield. It blocks the light and then reflects it back to its point of origin. Therefore, if the situation should arise in which you wish to make a thoughtform that would not only block a thought but send it back to the person sending it, you would make a thoughtform in the form of a shield that is also a mirror.

The symbols can be combined as well. Suppose you really want to get a thought through to Uncle Harry while he is busy with something. This is normally quite difficult, because the subconscious mind, which is where the psychic energy works best, cannot get through the noise generated by Uncle Harry's activity. You would in such an instance create two short-term thoughtforms. The first would be a rod coming from about six inches in front of your nose to the cup. The rod would be programmed to carry the message and the cup to receive it.

Now let us suppose that you are going to make a thoughtform that is going to be around for a while. These take a bit of work to make, not so much because they are long-lasting as because you have to keep feeding the little monsters in order to keep their power up. Never forget that any thoughtform is inherently unstable and will fall apart after a while. These thoughtforms can be the type that are used quite often, such as one made to keep your car out of accidents, or it may be one that is used only once a year.

The type that are used often are given a few good

charges and then a quick activation whenever needed. The mere fact of thinking that the thoughtform is activated puts energy into the thoughtform. The ones used less often have to be consciously charged over longer periods of time so that they can lie dormant until activated.

Let me give you examples of both. As I said, one of the most common of the standing thoughtforms is the one used to protect your car. It is a favorite with anyone who has to drive in heavy traffic, especially if the roads have a lot of taverns along them. This thoughtform is visualized best in the form of a shield over the car that emits a continuous light covering the entire car and in doing so keeps the car from meeting other cars, from being stolen or vandalized, or anything else. As the shield is supposed to last for a while, when it is being visualized give it a name, such as Carshield, or Fred. Each night for a week or two visualize the thoughtform over your car, shining its beacon, and program it something like this: "Your name is Carshield, and you will protect this car from anything that would injure it." After you have done this, each time you get into the car just think to the thoughtform the command, "Carshield, activate." The shield will power up and you will be able to drive with some certainty of your own safety. It is also a good idea to thank the thoughtform every time you miss getting clobbered. That will make the thoughtform happy and at the same time increase its power.

The other type is more on the order of a standing army. You may not wish to use it, but you would not want to be without it if you should need it.

Let us suppose that there is a particular resort that

you go to every summer. Now, as you have undoubtedly been made aware by those dreadful commercials showing happy vacationers losing their life savings, there is always some small risk that you may be robbed. You go to the resort often, so you can hold a picture of it in your mind with ease, or better still, you have a photograph of it. If that is the case, you may use your radionic box and psionic amplifying helmet to lock in on the resort, but it is not necessary. Visualization will do quite nicely. Either way, you will create another thoughtform, let us say in the form of a sword, which will drive away anyone who would desire to rob, injure or even annoy you. Then you name the thoughtform and charge it up every night for a couple of months before your vacation. You may then go off with peace of mind and enjoy your trip. But before you leave, you again visualize the thoughtform and tell it that it may rest until it is needed again. The next year, for about two weeks before your vacation, call up the thoughtform and renew the charge. Finally, before you arrive at the resort again, activate it. This thoughtform can be kept going virtually indefinitely.

You should now have all the information you need to make and use your own thoughtforms. There are a few more tricks that I will tell you about in the next chapter, but you now have all the basics and all you need is more practice. But suppose you wish to make a group thoughtform? You now know that it is very difficult to make such a thoughtform and expect it to hold together very well. After all, the more people that are working on it, the less effective it will be. Well, there is a way around this problem.

Let us take as our example the desire many people

have of creating a thoughtform that will bring world peace. They have a number of things working against them, not the least of these being that people are not really very peaceloving and are not likely to be for some time.

As I said, however, there is a way around this problem. Let's go back to Fatima for a minute. You will remember that the vision was strengthened not by the crowd concentrating on it, for they could not see it, but rather by the concentration of the crowd upon the children. The same principle applies here. A given individual can be chosen to make and charge the thoughtform, in whatever image he or she chooses, and then the rest of the people involved will concentrate their thoughts on him/her. The energy from these people will increase the power of his/her own, but because he/she is the only one who is putting energy into the thoughtform, the thoughtform will retain its coherence; thus the effect of the Principle of Ultimate Instability can be in large part overcome.

If you have a group of people (and this will be a small group, admittedly), you may use psionics to help you add power and coherence to your group thoughtform. Each member of the group will need a radionic box, a psionic amplifying helmet and a witness of the person who is to be the primary agent in creating the thoughtform.

You all must agree beforehand on a time for the creation and charging of the thoughtform. The person who is the primary agent must have a witness of each person in the group as well. Before the appointed time, the primary agent will place all of the witness samples in his or her radionic box and take what will be a general contact rate for the entire group. He/she will then also take such a rate on his/her helmet, which is of course linked to the box. Each member of the group, for their part, will take a contact rate for the primary agent.

At the appointed time, the primary agent will put on his/her helmet, placing him/her in firm contact with the rest of the group, and each member of the group will do the same. Thus, not only will a strong psychic link be established between the group and the agent, but a psionic link as well.

As the primary agent goes to work on the image he/she has chosen, the energy of the group will be transmitted to him/her without the usual drifting of contact, for the machines solve that problem. All anyone has to do is think. As their energy is fed into the prime agent, he or she, in turn, will put it into the thoughtform. This will create a thoughtform of tremendous coherence, and it will be able to cause events to occur far more effectively than the usual methods.

All this points to one simple and often overlooked fact of nature. No matter how strong a principle is, there is always a way around it, so if the laws of nature cannot be broken, they can certainly be bent.

There is one rule you should keep to if you are using a group to create a thoughtform. You must keep the group as small as possible. The more people involved, the more likely will there be someone who is not concentrating on the primary agent, or worse, sending conscious or unconscious thoughts counter to the purpose of the group. (This we will call counter-thoughtforming, and it has a real place in your repertoire, which I will explain later.) The tradition of keeping a coven to twelve or thirteen was undoubtedly created with this fact in mind. Even in the practice of a ritual, there is the danger that the ritual act will become so mechanical that only the most dedicated will be keeping their minds on the subject. For your purposes, therefore, I would recommend that you keep the number in your group to no more than eight. One of the more interesting things I learned in a beginner's course in sociology during my student days was that a primary group, a group in which everyone knows each other quite well and can function together most effectively as a unit, can have no more than eight members. After that it begins to break down into smaller groups, each with its own agenda, which may not be the same as that of the whole group. This may be one of the reasons why visions tend to stop after the crowds get too large. Once the trinket sellers move in, the concentration on the visionary is disrupted to the point where the coherence of the thoughtform falls apart, and the thoughtform with it.

Aside from using the machines, there are certain ritual practices that can be used to maintain a working thoughtform, though the study of this falls more under the heading of magick than of psionics. But as the two disciplines are related, the principles apply equally. The group must be kept small, if possible. If a large group is used, then the point of the thoughtform should be obvious to all involved. From that point, it is necessary to prevent the individuals from thinking too much, because then the coherency of the thoughtform is damaged.

For this reason it is best to have a specific target in mind, such as a sick person who needs healing. This will help keep minds from wandering. The other factor is speed. The faster a ritual is done, the less chance there is of stray thoughts entering and fouling the atmosphere. That is one of the reasons why in Tibetan practice mantras are repeated hundreds of thousands of times. The tremendous number makes it impossible to say them slowly and live to finish.

The complicated tables of correspondence used in ritual magick have much the same purpose. They require the participant to keep his or her mind on the object of the ritual. Therefore, in any ritual work the important things are to keep the thoughtform as objective as possible and to keep the participants as busy as possible. Avoid abstracts, and if the power can be focused on a given individual, so much the better.

PATTERNS
AND FORMS

In this chapter we are going to get into one of the stranger areas of psionics, and we will begin it with another little story. When John W. Campbell was experimenting with the seemingly miraculous Hieronymous Machine back in the early fifties, he stumbled on to something he considered truly phenomenal. He made a sort of circuit diagram of the machine (which looks like no circuit diagram I have ever seen) and attached some dials to it, and lo and behold! He still got a stick on the pad. This should be no surprise to you after working with your gauges, but it was quite a shock to Campbell, who apparently knew nothing about dowsing.

From this fact he made a deduction that it was the pattern of the machine, rather than the circuitry, that made it work. Of course, we know that it is neither, but let us not be nasty, for the fact is that pattern does play a huge role in psionics. There are a number of two-dimensional patterns, simple line drawings, that somehow interface with either the limited human or the less limited universal consciousness (and we do not know which) and produce profound psychic results.

This presents an unusual problem, for it is impossible to live without seeing patterns all around us.

If we assume that all of them are emitting some kind of energy into the ether, it can become very easy to be paranoid. Someone hears this idea at a lecture and immediately goes out and begins testing every line drawing that he or she sees, right down to the tile on his/her mother's floor, and before you know it convinces him/herself that all of them are in some way dangerous. Therefore, again I caution you, do not go to ridiculous extremes. Read the chapter and then experiment with an open mind, not an empty head.

You will remember that in *Psychic Power* I told the story of the psionic amplifying helmet and how it grew out of my dabbling with the Hills Magnetron device. That gadget, in its turn, had been the outcome of work begun by a pair of French radiesthesists named Servanx, who looked at a drawing of the innards of a radar device and held a pendulum over it. The pendulum spun, and thus they deduced that energy must be coming off it. You will also remember that the Magnetron pattern was a central circle, with eight circles around it connected to the center by eight lines. You can easily make such a drawing yourself.

The fascinating thing about the basic pattern of a central point surrounded by circles is that the more circles you have, the more powerful the energy coming off the center. You can prove this to yourself by making a number of such patterns, starting with three circles around the center one and going on from there. You may make as many as you wish, though I stopped at twelve because I was tired of making the patterns. The more circles you have, the more crowded the pattern gets, so I would suggest that you stop there. A twelve-circle pattern will look like Figure 9.

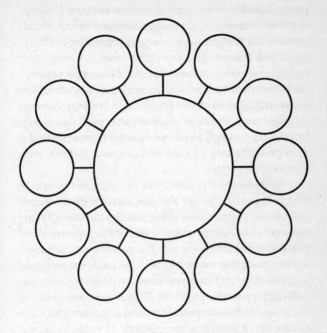

Figure 9

Once you have made your patterns, hold your pendulum over the center of each one. You will notice that they all produce a strong, clockwise swing. This is actually the first problem you will encounter in studying these things. The pendulum can tell you if an energy is coming off them and if the energy is positive (healthy) or negative (unhealthy), but it is useless in measuring the power of the energy. It always swings the same way, at least over these patterns. To learn anything else, you will need your gauge (numerical) and stick pad (the one you use to tune your helmet, with the plug and wire).

In these tests you will use the plug at the end of the pad wire as a probe and place it over the center of the pattern you are examining. Ask the question, "What is the level of energy coming out of the pattern?" and rub the stick pad as you use the pointer on the gauge. Write down the measurement for each pattern, and you will discover that you have a number of patterns with different energy levels. This means that you can use these to fine-tune the amount of power you wish to put into a psychic transmission. This can be useful in healing work, where too much energy might do more harm than good.

But what happens when we use such a pattern? Take a pencil and lay it along one of the lines. Have the point aim from the center of the large circle towards a smaller one. Now ask the stick pad if this is the direction that energy is flowing in. You will not get a stick, so the answer is no. Now reverse the pencil, so that it is pointed from a smaller circle to the large one, and ask the question again. This time you should get a stick. Therefore we can assume that each small circle is giving energy to the larger one, and the amount of energy coming out of the pattern is thus determined by the number of circles feeding it. So it does no good to place a witness on one of the outer circles.

These patterns may be used in several ways. The witness is always placed over the central circle.

If you wish to send a telepathic message to the subject, lay the witness in the pattern and hold your pendulum over the witness. Start the pendulum swinging around the pattern and think your message at the subject, repeating it until the pendulum stops swinging. At that point your subject should have received your message.

Colors may be transmitted to a subject by placing the gel over the witness and turning a light on it. Combined with transmittal patterns (we'll get to them soon), the color can be transmitted to any chakra or part of the body.

These patterns may also be used as simple energy amplifiers, to cause a subject to receive an increase in psychic energy or to increase the power of a thought-form. They have the advantage of never needing to be tuned, but the disadvantage of not being specific in the part of the subject you may wish to send to. For that you need either a very clear vision of the area or a transmittal pattern.

When being used as a simple energy amplifier, it is not always a good idea to leave the witness of a subject in the pattern. Its lack of specificity means that any emotion you may feel towards the subject will be amplified.

That might not seem like something of great

importance, but let us suppose that you are trying to send healing energy to your sick mother, and while her witness is in the pattern, she and you have a terrible argument as the result of the stress brought on by her illness. The anger that you release will be amplified by the pattern, and instead of helping her, you will make matters worse.

You can use any pattern that produces a clockwise swing in your pendulum for helping people. What you should avoid is any pattern that produces a counterclockwise swing. This sort of movement is exactly what you get if you hold a pendulum under a pyramid. It is the result of an etheric energy pattern that is known as "negative green."

Sounds pretty silly, does it not? Well, there is a reason for this rather odd terminology. It seems that a French radiesthesist discovered that this type of swing is exactly the opposite of the swing that he got over normal green on his color chart. That is why I instructed you to place gray opposite green on your color gauge. It is the swing that occurs over gray. And as it turns out, this energy is very bad stuff to have around. Let us be honest. Who really wants to become a mummy? Seriously, a lot of research has been done with this energy as its subject by various radiesthesists, and it seems to be extremely dangerous. One researcher, who wrote under the name of Enel, treated his patients for cancer by removing negative green from their etheric bodies, and he ultimately died of it himself. That could be an unfortunate coincidence, but it is wise not to take chances.

It is also true that the pendulum may swing in a counterclockwise direction for other reasons, so it is wise not to become paranoid. First look at the swing itself. If it is a very strong swing, assume that negative green is present until you can do another test. This is especially true of things such as crystals and running water. If you are going over a house and get this swing, there is usually a water pipe under the floor, in which case the energy is almost certainly negative green.

But if you are not sure, take your color gauge and stick pad and see what color the energy you are receiving corresponds to. If you get a stick on the gray, then you have negative green.

The clockwise swing, however, indicates an energy known as positive green, and this is quite healthy.

With that little digression out of the way, we can begin to look at patterns and their relationship to different energy fields around us and thoughtforms in particular. It is by the use of patterns that we can lock onto preexistent thoughtforms with great ease and increase the effectiveness of our own thoughtforms as well.

The idea that a two-dimensional pattern can link a person to the forces of the unseen world is hardly new. It is the basis for all talismanic magick. There are a number of these patterns that have come down to us, most notably the 72 sigils found in the Lesser Key of Solomon, the use of which was believed to enable the magician to control the demon whose sigil he or she possessed. What is clear is that these sigils can be used to cause certain results when used in conjunction with psionics. From this we can assume that in some way they align the operator or the subject with an energy pattern that already exists out in the void, and thus that pattern can be transmitted. These patterns exist for various purposes—from healing to wealth, love and destruction.

The seals in the Lesser Key (see Appendix 2) are among the easiest to use. They are already drawn, needing only to be copied and placed in the can. A rate is taken for the pattern and the witness is placed on the receiving end of the circuit. Once that is done, the chosen energy is sent to the subject. The only thing the operator need do is take the rate and then set up the machine. As the rates for these patterns never change, once it is recorded, all that is necessary to do is set up the box, look in the book of rates, and set the dials to the appropriate rate. The action is no more occult than turning on a light. In fact, it is so mechanical that it can become rather boring.

Of more interest, if only because it requires a bit more involvement, is the use of patterns drawn from magick squares and circle patterns. While the two methods are interchangeable and produce much the same results, I have found that each operation demands a choice of which to use. It may very well be a personal prejudice, but I use the magick squares to design patterns in those operations that would have fallen under the traditional heading of talismanic magick, and the circle patterns for those operations which do not. For example, if I am creating a love thoughtform, I would use a pattern drawn from a magick square, while a pattern to target energy to a certain part of the body would involve a circle pattern.

So how do we use these patterns? You begin by first determining what type of pattern you will need. After you have done this, you make the pattern and then the thoughtform. This may seem like a reversal of the usual procedure, but by making the pattern you are, in effect, laying the groundwork for the thoughtform, and thus your visualization becomes much easier.

So let us assume that you are going to make a thoughtform that has as its command, "Make everyone buy my book!" That is a bit of a mouthful for a pattern, so you choose a name for the pattern, in this case "Bestseller." And, as I wish to illustrate how both types of patterns are made, you choose to make it in the traditional manner using a magick square.

First you must choose which planet the thoughtform will correspond to. There are three possibilities that come to mind: the Sun, Mercury and Jupiter. This presents a bit of a problem, so you use your pendulum, and the pendulum tells you that Jupiter is the best planet for this particular project. Now I am going to give you another choice. The traditional method of working with magick squares requires that the letters of the words being used be broken down so that they correspond to single digits—1 to 9. For the smaller squares this works perfectly, as there are 26 letters in the English alphabet. But if you use the square for Venus, for example, it can be a real problem. This is because most of the numbers you would use are arranged in a diagonal row, which severely limits the number of patterns you can make.

Because of that difficulty, I decided to abandon tradition (which is about all most traditions are good for anyway) and use all 26 numbers, which means that it is not necessary to add down at all. The only drawback with this method is that you must have a square with more than five rows, otherwise numbers are going to be left out.

Jupiter has a square with four rows, so you have to use the oldfashioned technique.

First, you must find the value for each letter using a small chart like this:

```
1 2 3 4 5 6 7 8 9
a b c d e f g h i
j k l m n o p q r
s t u v w x y z
```

Then you find the value for each letter: B=2; E=5; S=1; T=2; S=1; E=5; L=3; L=3; E=5; R=9.

Now that you know the value for each letter, you take your square of Jupiter and plot the numbers on it.

4	14	15	1
9	7	6	12
5	11	10	8
16	2	3	13

Find the first number and draw a line between it and the second, the second and the third, and so on until you have run out of numbers. If you have a double number (3, 3 for L, L in this case), make a small curve between the first line going to the square and the line coming out of it. You will end up with a figure like this:

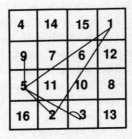

All that remains for you to do is to take a small piece of paper and trace the figure from the square onto it. It is a good idea to write the name of your thoughtform, in this case Bestseller, on the paper as well, so you will not forget what the pattern is supposed to represent.

Once you have done this, place the pattern in the

can of your radionic box and hook up your psionic amplifying helmet to the box input. Having done this, take a rate on both box and helmet for the pattern of your thoughtform. Record this rate, as it will not change.

Place the helmet on your head (which is where it is supposed to go anyway) and begin to make your thoughtform in the traditional manner—by visualizing it. The pattern is a witness for the thoughtform and may be left in the machine with a witness of the receiver (in this case an outer-space picture of the Earth works nicely), or it may be placed in the center of an amplifying pattern such as those you have just made. When you desire to add power to the thoughtform, you may either set up the box and helmet and visualize the thoughtform gaining energy or place it in the amplifying pattern and visualize it being charged while spinning the pendulum over it until the pendulum stops. Both systems work well, and you may have to do a bit of experimenting to see which one works better for you.

The circle patterns we are now going to work with have their origins in the work of Malcom Rae, who discovered that a pattern of lines inside a series of concentric circles would send his patients the energy equivalent of homeopathic remedies. By extension from this, patterns could be made that would be the equivalent of just about anything. These patterns could be used to eliminate rates in radionic broadcasting and analysis. We are not going to go quite that far. I still think the rate has its uses, but the circle patterns you are going to make will cause your work to become much easier. For example, in the older methods of radionic medicine, if a patient was to be cured of a heart ailment, the practitioner would first have to set a row of dials on his or her machine to the area affected and then set another row of dials to the curative rate. This meant that radionic machines had to be somewhat large and the procedure for treatment a bit complicated. With the aid of circle patterns, all that is necessary is to place a pattern for heart in the can with a witness of the subject and take a rate. The rate is then balanced as you learned to do in *Psychic Power*.

You can make circle patterns to correspond to any of the chakras, to any part of the body, and even to thoughtforms. They are particularly useful in working with preexisting thoughtforms and those thoughtforms created by other people. Circle patterns are also quite useful in working on specific parts and patterns in an individual's energy field, at any level.

So let us say that you wish to contact a big thoughtform, one that has been charged and recharged for thousands of years by innumerable people. You want to bring some of the energy from this thoughtform into your own etheric system and thus improve your lot in life. You want to tap into the power of Great Jehovah himself. No sense in thinking small, and so many different things have been put into this thoughtform that you can use it to energize just about anything.

The circle pattern you will use is much different from that used by the followers of Rae. It is a little easier to make, and I think it gives a better representation of the energies being contacted or used. You begin by drawing a circle that is marked off into segments of ten degrees (i.e., 36 hash marks) each.

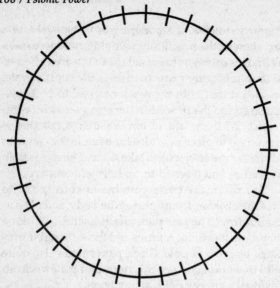

Try to make the circle no more than two inches in diameter. Any larger may create difficulties in fitting it into the sample can or onto a plate. It is also a good idea to make a sheet of these circles and then photocopy a bunch of them.

You will now need to get out your ruler and stick pad. Once you have them, write Great Jehovah over the top of the circle (not in the circle) and make a small dot over the topmost hash mark on the circle. That will be your starting point.

Concentrate on your thoughtform, trying to hold the idea of Great Jehovah in your mind, and point to the first hash mark while rubbing your stick pad. Slide your thumb across the pad about three or four times to see if you get a stick. If you do, make a small circle around the hash mark and go on to the next. If you do not, repeat the procedure with the next mark and continue until you have gone all the way around the circle. This should give you a pattern that looks something like this:

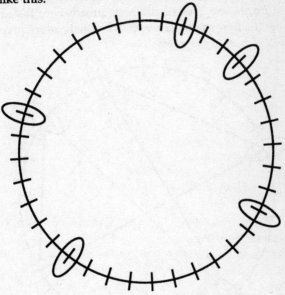

Once you have done this, take your ruler and lay it between the first and second small circle, on the hash marks. Ask yourself if you need a line between these points while rubbing the stick pad a few times. If you get a stick, draw the line. If not, place the ruler between the first and the third and repeat the procedure. Do this also if you get a stick, and repeat the procedure until you have tested the links between the first circle and all the others. Once you have finished, do this again with the second small circle until you have gone around the circle another time. Continue until you have tested all possible combinations, so that from the first circle you would have tested four possible lines; from the second, three; from the third, two; and from the fourth, one. The last circle has already been tested from the first, so you can stop. Your final pattern may look something like this:

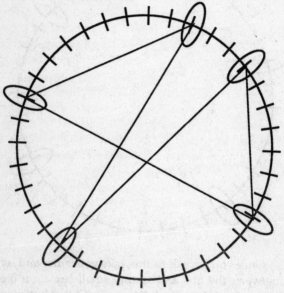

You now have a pattern that will automatically put you in mental contact with the humongous thought-form of Great Jehovah. Place this pattern in your radionic box, which you will have hooked to your psionic amplifying helmet. Take a rate on both and record it so that you can save yourself the trouble of taking the rate again, and place the helmet on your head.

Once you have the helmet on, you should begin to get a picture in your head of this thoughtform. Now I must explain that these things appear to each individual differently. I get something that looks like a cloud with the face of an elderly man on it, and the man has a long white beard, a *very* long white beard. Imagine as clearly as you can the energy from this thoughtform entering you and filling your being. This is a safe thoughtform to use for this, unlike some others that I will not name, lest some of my readers be tempted to try them. The most important thing to remember in these experiments is that you should always have some idea of the basic character of the thoughtform before you begin to work with it. That way you can save yourself some time, some embarrassment, and possibly great difficulty.

Having learned something about making circle patterns and using them to contact a preexisting thoughtform, you can now learn how to get a dose of healing energy and avoid having to give the Church a bundle of money at the same time.

In the last chapter we made hash of Fatima. Now we will do the same thing to Lourdes. The pattern of events was much the same: an adolescent, St. Bernadette, saw a vision, produced some phenomena, and as a result there is a giant, ever-recharging, healing thoughtform floating around the town, and, in particular, around the grotto where the visions took place and from where the stream of water associated with them first sprang. That water, incidentally, is said to be so polluted that it is truly a miracle that no one has become ill from it, so the thoughtform must work pretty well, and there are enough documented healings from that place to make working with it worthwhile.

The advantage of this particular thoughtform is that it is quite easy to work with. All you need do is go to the public library and make a photocopy of a photograph of the grotto. This should be found either in the travel section or under religion. When you get home, place this picture in your box and take a contact rate, as if you were going to do a remote viewing experiment. Once you have this rate on both box and helmet, put on the helmet and make a circle pattern that will correspond to the healing energy of that thoughtform. Clear the rate from the box and helmet and take a new rate for the thoughtform itself. You may now put the picture and the pattern in a safe place until they are needed.

Let us say that this time Uncle Harry has come down with triple pneumonia. Now is the perfect time to test your new tool. Place the picture and pattern in the sample can of your machine and set the dials for the thoughtform rate. Place the witness of Uncle Harry on the stick pad and let the machine work. The healing energy of the thoughtform will be transmitted to Uncle Harry and his recovery will be much aided by it. As you know from *Psychic Power*, however, I do not promise miracles. There are situations that even the most powerful thoughtform cannot handle, so if you should use this technique on someone who is dying and they go anyway, do not feel any guilt. At least you tried, and that is more than most people are willing or able to do.

I have used Lourdes as an example here because it is one of the best-known sites for thoughtform tapping, but it is certainly not the only one. Any location associated with healing, or any psychic or spiritual activity can be used. The technique is always the same. Use a pattern in conjunction with the box and helmet, and draw the energy into yourself or transmit it to your subject.

The only caution I would give in the use of these thoughtforms is to make sure you know something about the deity you are going to use, otherwise you may be in for an unpleasant shock. Always know what you are getting into, or more importantly, what is getting into you.

GADGETS AGAIN

What would a book about psionics be without some new toys to play with? Up to now, except for a few gauges, you have not had the opportunity to make anything new. Well, now we are going to change that situation.

If you will think back to *Psychic Power*, you will remember that the energy we use has certain properties, among them the ability to be carried along beams of light and electromagnetic carrier waves, such as radio and microwaves. I will give you some advice on how to use this fact for your advantage, by increasing the power of your radionic transmissions.

You will need to have a cassette recorder (the oldfashioned monaural type is best), an FM radio with an external antenna, and cheap, 100 mW walkie-talkies available from any toy store. This last should have retractable antennae.

One of the peculiar things about radionics is that an amplified current can aid in the output of the mechanism. It seems to give a little more push to the energies being used, and there are two ways that this current can be used. The current can be put through the radionic box, thus energizing the entire system, or a carrier wave may be added after the box, thus giving

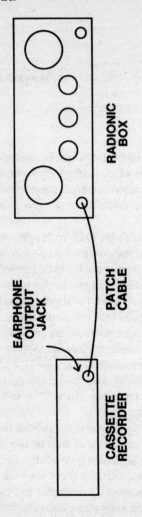

RADIONIC
BOX

PATCH
CABLE

EARPHONE
OUTPUT
JACK

CASSETTE
RECORDER

Figure 10

an added impetus to the completed transmission. You will have to experiment to find out what method works best for you, but I have usually used the first method when transmitting patterns to a subject and the second when transmitting with the helmet, so if I were going to use the helmet and box to send a message to someone, I would add the light or the carrier wave to the end of the system rather than to the beginning.

The recorder is placed in the system as shown in Figure 10. When doing this, the pattern, witness and rate have already been placed on the machine and the recorder is connected from the earphone jack to the left-hand jack of the box. There is no need to have a tape in the recorder; in fact, it is best not to have one, at least at this point. Simply turn on the recorder in playback and set the volume control by rubbing the stick pad while turning it, just as if you were taking a rate. In fact, you are taking a rate, and if the volume control is calibrated, it is a good idea to mark it down in your book of rates. The recorder can be left on as long as you wish and the machine can stand, though I have found it convenient to turn the recorder off before I go to bed at night.

Using the FM radio is a bit more complicated, as Figure 11 shows. You will need, in addition to the radio, a length of wire with an alligator clip on each end, a foil plate (made by gluing a square of aluminum foil over a square of cardboard), and a patch cable to attach the radio to the box.

Begin by taking a rate on the box for the pattern that you wish to transmit. You will find that the radio is used best with transmittal patterns and the recorder with balancing rates. Once you have done this, use the

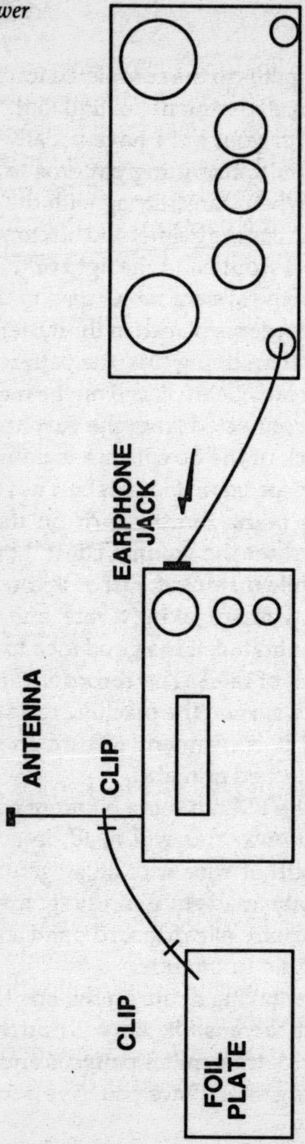

ANTENNA

CLIP

CLIP

FOIL PLATE

EARPHONE JACK

Figure 11

wire with the clips to attach the foil plate to the antenna of the radio. Place the pattern on the plate and attach the radio to the box by means of the patch cable. Now use the stick pad to take a rate for the pattern on the radio the same way as you did the box. It is best to work the volume control first, then the tuner, and finally the tone controls. It is also a good idea to make sure that you have set the radio to FM. When you forget this, the rate may still work but you will feel really silly.

Plug in the radio, if it is not already, and the energy from the radio will increase the output of your machine. You may verify this by testing the output of your box on your numerical gauge, and then add the radio and test again. You will also notice from experience that amplification does help at times.

It has been awhile since I gave you an example, so you will not mind if I throw one in now. A few years ago, I was interested in a young lady and I was getting nowhere. Well, I came to the conclusion that a little boost was needed, so I set up the box for a contact rate for the subject and set up the radio for the rate of a transmittal pattern appropriate to the operation. I plugged in the radio and let fly. When I saw the woman a few days later the change was dramatic, and she has been my good friend ever since.

Modifying a walkie-talkie for use with a radionic device takes a little more work, but it is well worth the trouble. This gadget is usually added to the system after the box, so that the signal coming out of the box is transmitted over the radio carrier wave. For this reason it is best to use a walkie-talkie with an adjustable antenna, which can be made very short, because the FCC gets

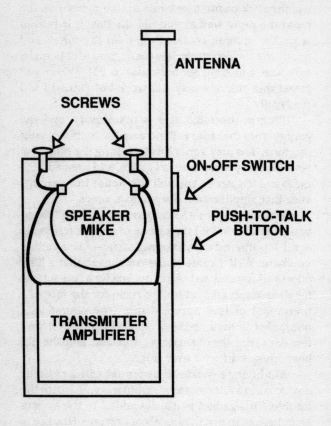

Figure 12

very upset at people who disrupt radio traffic. A shortened antenna will allow the wave to go out, but it will
not be strong enough to be picked up by any but the
most sensitive equipment.

Please take the above instruction very seriously.
Avoid the temptation to lengthen the antenna. It has
little effect on the results, and I would be unhappy if
one of my readers ended up in jail.

You will see in Figure 12 that a walkie-talkie, at
least the cheap variety, uses the speaker for a micro-
phone. The speaker is wired into the transmitter from
two small tabs on the back of the speaker, so when you
take apart the radio, you must get at those tabs. This is
usually quite easy, the speaker often being laid between a few slots and simply lifted out, but sometimes
you must remove some small screws to take it out.
Once you have the speaker out, do not disconnect the
speaker from the amplifier. Having the speaker still in
the system makes testing the battery easy.

Drill two small holes in the top of the walkie-
talkie case. It is best to use a hand drill for this, as a
power drill might push too hard and damage the
transmitter. Place two screws in the holes, and wire
each screw to a tab on the speaker.

Put the walkie-talkie back together and tape down
the push-to-talk button. This way the walkie-talkie
will always transmit when you turn on the power
switch.

This device is usually used when you want a
burst of power for a short period of time. The life of the
battery is limited.

In order to wire the box, or helmet, to the walkie-
talkie, you will need a special patch cable with a plug

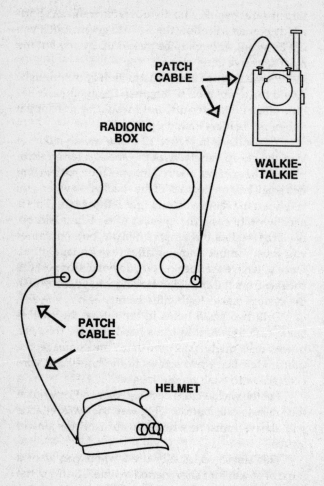

PATCH CABLE

RADIONIC BOX

WALKIE-TALKIE

PATCH CABLE

HELMET

Figure 13

on one end and two alligator clips on the other. Each clip is attached to one of the screws, and when you transmit, the signal from the box or helmet is sent through the screws into the transmitter and thence out into the void or to your target, depending upon the nature of the operation.

The addition of a carrier wave can be a great benefit in most communication experiments. There are a number of ways this can be done.

The helmet can be directly connected to the walkie-talkie. In this case, the rate is only on the helmet, and no witness sample is used once the rate has been taken. It is difficult to judge the difference in performance with this method because it is necessary that the operator hold a clear image of the subject in his or her mind while transmitting.

Far better is the use of the helmet and box along with the walkie-talkie. In this case, it is not necessary to hang onto the image of the subject. The box and helmet lock in on that for you. All that is required is that the equipment be set up and you can transmit with relative ease (Figure 13).

Those of you who have been diligent in your study of *Psychic Power* can probably guess what is going to come next. And you are right. For once you have set up your equipment in this manner, the next step is to add your teleflasher (see Appendix 4). The operator has now put together an impressive array of machinery that will have a tremendous impact on the person to whom he or she is transmitting, provided he/she is careful not to make the mistake I did once.

One evening I was using my equipment in much the same manner as I am telling you now. Unfortunately I had made the terrible mistake of leaving my door open, and at that moment my mother walked by and saw her son, whom she still had illusions of being sane, wired into his machinery. In a matter of seconds she was laughing so hard that she could barely stand up, and you know how catching laughter is. The experiment ended neither with a bang nor with a whimper, but rather in a veritable gale of hilarity. I was never able to get my mother to take this stuff seriously.

But all this leads to an obvious question, namely, why would the addition of a radio carrier wave or an amplified current affect psychic transmission? It is a hard question to answer, and please do not think that I have the last word on it. What I am giving you is nothing more than my best guess.

It all comes down to the peculiar relationship between electromagnetic energy and the psychic wave. Even as the psychic wave is produced by the relationship between the electrical activity in our brains and the various levels of the etheric body, so it is made more powerful by the addition of electromagnetic energy, as in using light to boost a radionic signal. Unfortunately, we are not able to accurately describe the full nature of this relationship, and thus we are going to be left with a mystery for others who are far better thinkers than I to solve. I wish them luck.

But suppose that you wish your transmission to be more effective still. You already know that the teleflasher can work (in conjunction with radionic equipment) because of the effect of rhythmic flashing on the brain of the sender. By adding the same rhythm to the radio transmission, the receiver will also be thus affected.

There are two ways to accomplish this. The first way is to cut one of the wires leading from the battery clip to the amplifier of the walkie-talkie. A button, like that of a doorbell, is wired into the system by means of a long wire (Figure 14). When you sit before the teleflasher, each time the image is lit, you push the button. This will set up a rhythm in the brain of the receiver and increase the ability of your message to get through the noise that is usually occupying the mind of anyone we wish to send to. In fact, getting

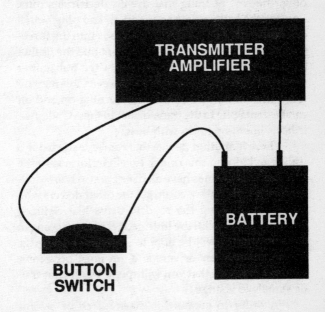

Figure 14

through this noise is one of the principal difficulties that face any who work in the area of the psychic. People tend to be very inconsiderate and refuse to leave their minds totally empty for us. It can become quite annoying at times, and you would be amazed at the amount of garbage that can fill the thoughts of even the stupidest of humans.

My little tirade over, I am sure you are anxious to learn the other method. It is even easier than the first, though it can be a bit hard on the equipment.

You will need an AC adapter and a three-way plug, the sort of thing that drives electricians nuts. Replace the battery with the adapter, and plug both it and the light cord from the flasher box into the three-way plug. Now plug this arrangement into the flasher plug. Each time the teleflasher lights, the transmitter will go on for a second. As I said, however, this method has a drawback. The continuous turning on and off can be damaging to the transformer in the AC adapter. It has something to do with heat.

There is another device that can be made using a walkie-talkie, and this one is excellent for use in the car. How many times have all of us been in heavy traffic and wished that we could get the other drivers who insist on crowding the road to drive like civilized human beings? With the little gadget you are going to build now, you will be able to safely get a message across to the other drivers and, on most occasions, decrease the time that you will spend waiting for traffic signals to change.

In order to create this masterpiece of psionic ingenuity, you will need a piece of foil, a plastic box such as the type sold for schoolchildren to keep their pencils in, a switch, some wire, and glue.

Go back to the chapter on patterns and make one with the large central circle surrounded by smaller circles. You have to decide how many small circles you will want to have in this pattern, but I suggest a minimum of seven. Once you have made the pattern, trace it onto the foil and cut it out. Lay this to one side where it will not get crumpled.

Now take apart the walkie-talkie. Be certain that you use the correct size screwdrivers, because some of the screws can be quite small, and you do not wish to damage anything when you remove the circuitry from the case. You may have some trouble with the antenna arrangement, so be patient, work slowly, and do a neat job. Once you have finished with this task, lay the chassis of the walkie-talkie near your pattern and dispose of the case.

Take the plastic box and punch two small holes in the top. Make a small coil of wire, small enough to lay flat under the central circle of your foil pattern, and run the two ends through the holes in the box. Glue the foil pattern over the coil, making sure that all the wire is covered by the coil. When you lay your fingers over the central circle, they should also be over the center of the coil.

Punch more holes in the side of the box for the switch and the antenna. Now cut the speaker wire away from the chassis, leaving enough wire to make a good connection. Cut one of the battery wires as well.

Mount the chassis inside the box. This can be done either by screwing it down, if possible, or merely taping it securely in place with plastic tape. Be sure

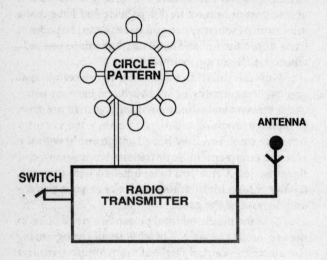

Figure 15

that the power switch of the walkie-talkie is turned on when mounting, and tape or wire down the push-to-talk button.

Attach the wires from the coil to the speaker wires. Mount the on-off switch to the outside of the box and connect it to the battery wire that you have cut (Figure 15). Attach a wire to the antenna connection and run it out through the provided hole in the box. Now close the lid. It sounds more complicated to make than it really is, and except for removing the chassis of the walkie-talkie from its case, it should take you very little time.

So how is this machine used? When you are driving, place this box on the seat beside you. It is a good idea to leave the power off, because otherwise you will go through a lot of batteries. As you come up to a stoplight, turn on the power and place the index and middle fingers of your right hand on the center of the circle pattern. Will the light to either turn or stay green, depending upon the situation. The results will vary somewhat, but at least half of the time it should change immediately and another 30 percent of the time it will change more quickly. Of course, there are those days when nothing seems to work, so do not become discouraged if nothing happens.

You can also use this machine for simple communication experiments, particularly in getting other drivers to move. I am sure you can think of plenty of uses for this machine.

Now let us consider using light for a while. You will remember from earlier chapters that adding light to a radionic transmission had a clear effect upon the receiver of that transmission. And it is true that a light beam can be used to increase the effectiveness of any psychic work. You may prove this to yourself with the aid of a friend.

Have your friend sit with his or her back to you, holding a pendulum over a chart with the letters of the alphabet written on it around a half circle. Think a letter at him/her and find out how long it takes for the pendulum to swing to that letter. Mark down the time and then repeat the experiment with one small change. While thinking of a letter, shine a flashlight on the back of your friend's neck, over the throat chakra. You should notice a marked improvement in the speed of the response and the strength of the pendulum swing.

There is really only one problem in using light to aid psychic transmission, and that is getting the energy to run along the light beam. When you are holding a flashlight this is not difficult, for you visualize the message being carried by the light, but when you are working with a group of psionic devices at once, that can be difficult, if not impossible. Fortunately there is a way around this difficulty as well.

You will need a small, high-intensity lamp, a sheet of posterboard, aluminum foil, and two screws with four nuts. Cut a square from the posterboard large enough to make a tube or sleeve that will fit over the end of the lamp, so that the light from the lamp will be directed through the sleeve. Cut a piece of foil that will cover one side of the posterboard and glue it into place. Punch two holes in this sheet and be certain that the screws fit them without being too loose.

You will probably be wondering why I instructed you to have four nuts for two screws. When the tube is complete, you will not want the screws to be sliding in and out, therefore screw one nut on each screw before inserting it in its hole. Then place the other nut on the inside, over the foil, and tighten it to hold each screw in place. This will cause the head of each screw to stand up slightly when the tube is complete.

Roll up the tube with the foil inside and fit it over the end of the lamp. Glue or tape it together, and it should look something like Figure 16. Attach this over the end of the lamp.

To use this piece of equipment, attach the tube to either your helmet or your machine by means of the cable with the alligator clips holding the screws. The witness of the person you are transmitting to is then placed in the beam of light from the lamp. As you

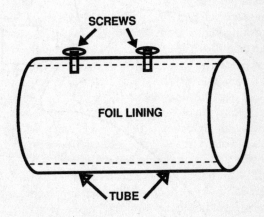

Figure 16

transmit, the energy of your thought is picked up by the beam of light from the foil and shot at the witness and thence to the subject. The rates used are the same as in ordinary transmission—contact rate for telepathy, and pattern rate for transmittal pattern. This device is rarely, if ever, used with a balancing rate.

The sleeve may also be adapted to a flashlight to be used with the helmet as a portable unit, though I admit that I do not have the nerve to use something like that myself.

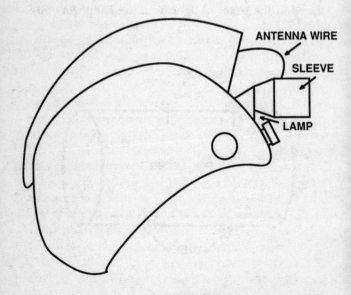

Figure 17

A version of the above method can be adapted to the helmet itself to make a self-contained unit. You will need a psionic amplifying helmet with the crest opened in front, a headband lamp (sold in camping stores), and a light-tube.

As you can see from Figure 17, the lamp is mounted just above the dials of the helmet. This may take some doing, and you may have to remove the strap from the lamp and use mounting brackets to hold it in place, depending upon the shape of your helmet. The important thing is that the lamp be fitted securely. The sleeve is then mounted over the end of the lamp, and a wire is attached from the antenna inside the crest to the tube. One word of caution. When mounting the lamp, make sure that you can change the batteries.

There is one more gadget that you can make with a light which you may find useful. It has the advantage of being portable, and it can be used with the helmet as well.

After *Psychic Power* came out, I was asked by a number of readers why I did not include any gadgets with quartz crystals. There were two very good reasons for this. The first was that at the time *Psychic Power* was being written, I did not have ready access to crystals and thus had not had any opportunity to experiment with them. The second was that my publisher already had a good book out on the subject, *Crystal Power*, and there seemed no point in duplicating what was in that book. Well, a couple of years have passed since then, and as crystals have become more popular, it has become easier to get them and thus I am able to give plans for this simple device.

As you can see from Figures 18 and 19, it is a pro-

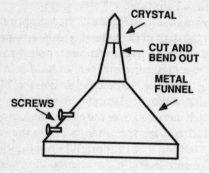

Figure 18

gression from the light-tube and requires a six-volt flashlight, a metal funnel, a small quartz crystal, and two screws. It works on the same principle as the tube, the light taking the thought energy from the funnel and then energizing the crystal.

Following the pattern in Figure 18, take the funnel and punch two small holes for the screws and cut four short slots at the narrow end of the funnel. Bend these out and fit the crystal with the pointy end facing outward, and apply a small amount of instant glue to the crystal. Bend the funnel end back in to make a tight fit, and let the glue set for a little while.

Fit the screws into the small holes, and glue the funnel arrangement onto the end of the flashlight, as in Figure 19. When in use, the patch cable is attached

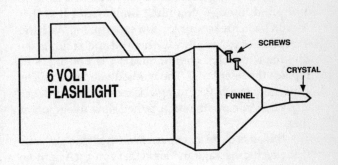

Figure 19

to the screws, as in using the walkie-talkie, and the lantern turned on. The crystal will act as the signal amplifier, and there is no need to point the device directly at a witness sample.

The devices I have described in this chapter are designed mostly for communication work. In other words, you have a message of some sort that you wish to send to a person by psychic means, and these devices increase the ability of the message to get through the noise. So let us say that you wish to send a normal message to someone who has had the great blessing of having also built these machines. All well and good, though you must understand that this should be in the nature of a fun experiment. With the exception of extremely experienced and accurate individuals, psychic communication is not likely to replace the telephone. The method you are going to experiment with, for example, is more on the order of a psychic telegraph, and a rather slow telegraph at that.

Still, it is quite an experience when you get your first psychic message and learn that you got it right, so do not be afraid to give it a try. You will need to decide who will transmit and who will receive. The transmitter will need at least a psionic amplifying helmet, a radionic box, a teleflasher, and a witness of the receiver. He or she may also wish to add either the walkie-talkie or a crystal or light-tube amplifier to his/her system. The receiver will need only a psionic amplifying helmet, a radionic box, a pendulum, and alphabet chart or a ouija board. The ouija board is faster.

It is necessary to agree on a time for the experiment to take place. It will do no good for one person to be merrily beaming away and the receiver watching television. Both should have their equipment set up and ready. The transmitter should have a series of cards or pieces of paper with the letters of the alphabet on them handy.

At the appointed time the receiver will take up his/her position with either pendulum or board, and the transmitter will begin to send his/her message, one letter at a time. At this point there may be a little problem, for the transmitter will have little way of knowing if the letter has been received, and he/she may go on to the next. There are two ways around this difficulty. First, the transmitter can set an arbitrary time limit for the sending, such as one minute for each letter. Second, he/she may use his/her pendulum to tell him/her when the letter has been received. To do this, the pendulum is held next to some upright object, such as the side of the table or inside a glass, and allowed to swing. When it hits the side, the message has gotten through, and you may go on to the next.

It is also a good idea to agree on a code, such as *N* to signify a new word, and *end* to signify the end of the message. After all, you would not wish your receiver to be sitting there all night waiting for the rest of the message.

There is one other little matter that I should caution you about, though in most cases it will not really matter. Telepathic transmission, particularly of this type, is not exactly confidential. Anyone who has the equipment, a witness sample of the transmitter, and the time of transmission (which can be dowsed for if the other things are available) can pick up the message as well. There are no forms of communication more easily intercepted than psychic ones, so do not count on secrecy.

Of course, this fact has a good side to it. Suppose that you wish to create a demand for a certain product in the mind of the mass of consumers. You no longer need to spend large amounts on advertising. All that is needed is a photo of the product, your transmittal equipment and a space-picture of the Earth. You set up your equipment with the Earth itself as the receiver witness and begin to flash the picture of your product to sleeping humanity. Any message that you may wish to send to large numbers of people can be sent in this way. Or you may wish to tailor your market to a specific town. In that case you would acquire an aerial photograph of the town and broadcast to it at a time when the populace is asleep.

PSYCHIC CONFLICT

In this chapter we are concerned with the conflicts of daily living and the occasional feud between angry psychics. Almost all books on the subject of psychic conflict cover it from the standpoint of "psychic self-defense." This is a point of view with which I strongly disagree. Wars are not won by going on the defensive, and you must view psychic conflict, if you should ever become involved in it, as a war in which no prisoners are taken and no quarter ever offered the fallen. The other way of looking at this sort of thing is to have the person hide behind a sort of psychic "Maginot Line" and let the attacker exhaust himself.

This sort of thinking does not always work in the case of real warfare. And we can find the best examples of it not working in history as well as in psychic combat.

Let us go back in time to the First World War. For those of you who do not know, in 1914 there was a minor disagreement between Austria-Hungary and Serbia over the little matter of an assassination involving the heir to the Austro-Hungarian throne. In a very short time, Austria-Hungary had declared war on Serbia, Russia had declared war on Austria-Hungary, Germany had declared war on Russia and France had declared war on Germany. Germany invaded Belgium to get to France, and the British, incensed at the thought of such a foul deed, declared war on Germany to make the world safe for waffles.

The armies marched around for a while, turning Europe into a wasteland and blowing Flanders completely off the map. (Have you ever tried to find Flanders on a map?) Then somebody decided to dig a trench, and before you could say "poppies," there were trench lines running from the North Sea to the Swiss border. (The Swiss were the only ones to keep their heads in this whole silly affair.) The war settled down to a conflict of sieges, each side trying to break through the other's lines while holding their own, and nobody got anywhere. So for a couple of years there was a war that produced nothing but a lot of dead people and some of the worst poetry ever written.

Meanwhile, both sides were playing with new aircraft, and the British were inventing a machine called a tank to break through the barbed wire that now enforested the battlefields. In the United States, the home of barbed wire, it was decided to enter the war against Germany to make the world safe for democracy, though it is beyond me what democracy has to do with waffles.

Thus in 1918 the defensive war gave way to an offensive one. The Germans broke through the French and British lines and nearly took Paris, and the British, French and a relative handful of Americans smashed through the German lines. The Balkan front collapsed, and Germany and Austria-Hungrary, exhausted by the fighting, gave up. Peace was declared and everyone went home to get ready for the next fight. The

British and the Germans perfected their tanks and short-range aircraft, the Americans worked on long-range aircraft and ships to carry them, as did the Japanese, and only the French learned virtually nothing from the Great War.

Determined that the barbarous Germans should never again set foot upon the sacred Gaulish soil, they set to work building a super defense line of fortresses. This was the Maginot Line, and it proved very good for hanging out the washing but useless for anything else. You see, the French had forgotten a lesson that goes back to the Romans, a lesson that has great value for anyone who studies psychic combat: A defensive position is useful only as a springboard for an offense. When the next war came, the Germans simply skipped past the Maginot Line, and attacked from the rear.

The point of this little digression is to persuade you of a simple fact. There is no defense that cannot be penetrated, and anyone who is foolish enough to hide behind a "strengthened aura" or other such nonsense is in for a terrible surprise if he or she should be up against someone who is really serious about psychic attack.

So let us look at psychic combat. History has a number of legends concerning it, but little hard evidence; therefore I am going to tell you a story of psychic warfare that will illustrate the sort of tales that grow up around this stuff and also show you what not to do.

Our subject is the Tibetan sage Milarepa. While but a boy, Milarepa's father died and his paternal uncle, a truly nasty fellow, laid claim to Milarepa's father's lands, driving the young lad and his mother and sister from their home and virtually reducing them to the state of beggars. As you may well imagine, this caused no small amount of bitterness in the family, and Milarepa's mother awaited the day when her son would be old enough to wreak vengeance on his uncle.

That time finally came when Milarepa, now a young man full of energy and desire, went forth from his village to seek a guru who would instruct him in the art of killing evil relatives. His travels finally caused him to encounter two other seekers after power who were going to study under a famous sorcerer known as Lama Yungtun-Trogyal, which translates as "Wrathful and Victorious Teacher of Evil."

This worthy scholar accepted young Milarepa as a pupil, and together with his fellow students, he was taught certain rituals and methods of Tibetan magic which, while satisfying his fellows, left young Milarepa with the feeling that something had been left out. When the time came for the students to leave and return to the outside world, Milarepa stayed behind, telling his teacher that he was certain there was more to be learned from him, adding that if he returned to his mother unable to complete his appointed task she would probably kill herself in his presence.

The teacher was greatly impressed with the zeal of this one student and sent another pupil, who was as swift as a horse and as strong as a yak, to Milarepa's home village to see if the story concerning his mistreatment by his uncle was true. In due course the spy returned with corroborating evidence, and the teacher agreed that Milarepa was deserving of further instruction, being almost moved to tears by the tale of injustice.

There was only one small difficulty in furthering the education of the young sorcerer. It seemed that the secret of destroying large numbers of people was no longer available to the Wrathful and Victorious Teacher. He had, some years ago, given it to a close friend, and it was to that teacher that Milarepa would have to go.

So off he went. Upon arriving at his new instructor's home, he presented a letter detailing his request and an introduction from his former guru. The new teacher was also much moved by the tale of suffering and immediately agreed to begin instructing the young Milarepa.

Milarepa was instructed to build a hermitage for his operations, and then taught what was necessary for his work (the details of which are left out of the biography, obviously lest someone else use them without paying his guru).

The operations should normally have taken seven days, but as the target village was some distance, Milarepa asked for seven additional days. The teacher, unwilling to hurt his pupil's feelings by explaining to him that the deities being summoned did not travel by yak, allowed this, and on the fourteenth day his work was rewarded by a vision of the deities bringing him a gift of 35 heads and hearts. A day later the deities returned and said that there were two that had escaped and asked if Milarepa desired them killed as well. Milarepa, thinking that by leaving these two alive fear of him would be spread far and wide, told the deities to leave them unharmed. The two happened to be his aunt and uncle, precisely the ones he wanted to kill in the first place.

On the same day Milarepa completed his operation, the eldest son of his uncle was about to be married. The wedding feast was packed with his uncle's friends and supporters, his other sons, and the bride. In short, all of the worst enemies of Milarepa were present in the house. A maid went out to fetch some water and ran in fright as the animals went berserk, with the result being that a horse kicked out one of the main pillars supporting the house and the whole thing fell down, killing all inside except the aunt and uncle.

Upon seeing the disaster, Milarepa's mother was seized with a fit of joy, and making a makeshift flag, ran around the village shouting the praises of her son the sorcerer. This act, for obvious reasons, did not exactly endear her to those who lost family in the wreckage, and their response could be summed up in two words: "Kill her!"

This may well have occurred had not cooler heads realized that her son, who was the cause of all the trouble, might not look with favor upon such action, and thus the cry was changed to "Kill him first!" As finding Milarepa would take some time, all plans of retaliation were put off, and Milarepa's mother took advantage of the lull in the fighting to send a message to her son warning him of the danger and asking him to cause such a disaster that the village would never forget it.

Milarepa received the warning and showed it to his teacher, who remarked that Milarepa had a very unpleasant mother. But Milarepa needed a more powerful spell and thus he was sent back to Wrathful and Victorious. This teacher welcomed his old, and possibly best, student with open arms and proceeded to teach Milarepa the art of making hailstones, an ancient Tibetan custom.

With another pupil as an assistant, the one who had been sent to determine the truth of Milarepa's story, the young sorcerer, disguised as a pilgrim, returned to a hill overlooking his old village. On the top of the hill he set up his apparatus. It was a moment he had waited some time for. His teacher asked him how high the barley would be, and when told it was just starting to grow, instructed Milarepa to wait. Again the question was asked, and again, waiting was enjoined. But then came the time when the barley crop, upon which the entire village depended for its winter food supply, was ready to be harvested.

So the barley fields awaited the reapers, but before the grain could be harvested, Milarepa performed his operation and the sky opened with three massive hailstorms, so powerful that all the barley was destroyed and the village faced a long, hungry winter. The fact that his mother and sister would share in the general distress apparently did not concern Milarepa. After this rip-roaring success, Milarepa returned to his teacher, and instead of pursuing what could have been a very lucrative career as a sorcerer, decided to attain enlightenment and become a saint. It was just as well because his mother, who instilled the desire for revenge in her son, did not much profit by it, becoming an outcast (guess why); and his sister, whom no one would marry (hardly surprising, considering the in-laws) and faced with the somewhat limited options open to women in eleventh-century Tibet, became a wandering beggar. As I said, Milarepa did not seem to be very bright.

I have told this story at length because it is an

excellent illustration of the traditional form of psychic warfare and, while showing its strength, also gives a good indication of those things to avoid, chief among them being a tendency to overkill.

While the operations of Milarepa were successful on their face, they ultimately proved to be costly failures. Why? First, his mother was cursed with a hyperactive tongue. Second, he totally failed to tailor his actions to the requirements of the situation. He killed everyone but the very people he was aiming at and ended up starving his mother and sister. Now the mystically minded would say that such was the result of "karma." Baloney! It was the result of stupidity. It would be the equivalent of nuking Denver for a parking ticket in Seattle.

For their parts, the people of the village were also foolish, for upon hearing that Milarepa had gone to learn the methods of revenge, they should have seen to their defenses and perhaps launched a preemptive strike. But nothing was done. It is one thing to avoid paranoia, but quite another entirely to leave the door open and a neon sign that says "Burglars Welcome."

So before we get technical, let us look closely at the difference between rational prudence and paranoia. It is a distinction of great importance, often overlooked by those who study psychic combat.

We must first understand that no one goes through life without making people mad on occasion. We know that each time a strong emotion is felt, it gives off a wave of energy into the ether, and this wave can be felt by its target. But most of the time the emotion is so incoherent that even if felt, it can have no ill effect. There is a lot of unpleasant emotion floating around, and the fact is that anyone in reasonably good mental health should not be bothered by it at all. In fact, as far as self-defense goes, the best way to deal with the usual murk of thoughtforms is by having a good laugh, at least once a day, and once an hour if possible.

This is lost on some authors, who would have their readers convinced that everyone is out to get them and thus set them to work creating defensive fields and strengthened auras and whatnot, all with the aim of protecting them from the office gossip! One writer even went so far as to describe in vivid detail the experience of a student of his who awoke to witness a veritable gunfight on the lower astral as his protective thoughtform exchanged bolts of cosmic lightning with an attacking thoughtform. It is amazing that the students of this man are able to get out of bed in the morning without being terrified of the anger they may create by the noise of their waking!

We are not going to waste our time on such nonsense. In point of fact, it is unlikely that you will ever need to worry too much about this sort of thing. Unless someone has paid a witch doctor or you have angered a kahuna, you are unlikely to need a high order of defensive paraphernalia. Still, this stuff can be good to know, as long as you do not worry that your barber is selling your hair clippings to a disgruntled employee.

Remember my comments about World War One. No defense can be built that cannot be penetrated. Therefore, if you should feel the need to build a defensive system, always keep that fact in mind. I never erect a defense without creating an offensive capability as well.

Before you begin to consider defense at all, you should first decide if you need one. Just because the horses are not running well for you these days does not mean that a curse is on you. You may just need a new bookie. Seriously, people have gone to the funny farm because they became convinced that someone was psychically zapping them, so do not get all worried about something without proof.

Admittedly, proof of psychic attack is rather hard to find, as most of us who have launched one will count on. A good rule to follow before even considering the possibility of such an attack being aimed at you is to look at the degree of difficulty that you find yourself in, the strangeness of that difficulty and any other odd things that might lead to the conclusion that someone is making you the target of a psychic attack. In other words, everyone has an occasional bad dream, but if you have the same nightmare for eight days in a row, you might consider checking for a psychic attack. If you wake up to terrible smells in your room, and you know that the cat is not hiding its mice under your bed, then you had better look for a psychic attack; and if things start flying around the room, run like hell, because I do not think that even I know how to deal with that.

Seriously, it is highly unlikely that you would ever encounter the more extreme forms of psychic assault. They tend to be more the stuff of legend than reality. And the most important thing that you can do is to avoid paranoia, for as the saying goes, "Those whom the gods would destroy, they first make mad."

But let us suppose that you have good reason to think that someone is singling you out for a psychic bombardment. Perhaps you have offended the neighborhood sorcerer, or you have received a letter from a deranged ex-lover telling you that he or she is praying for your early demise. Take such threats with some seriousness, but do not get overly worried about them. The normal form of psychic assault is relatively easy to defend against.

You have in your etheric body the basic building materials of your psychic fortification. It is so designed that most of the thoughts of those around us cannot penetrate at all, and while we may feel their emotions if strong enough, they are rarely able to damage anyone in good health. You have to be in pretty bad shape to be injured by even the most determined emotional blast. You may get a little irritable but that seems to be the extent of it. Therefore, to oppose such offensives, all you need do is set up a wave pattern, or waveform, in your etheric body that will block any such attacks while covering your counter-blow. This last is of great importance. Never let any attack go unanswered. Always shoot back. Remember that any defense is only useful in that it provides a base for an offensive.

So let us set up your defense pattern. Meditate, and while meditating visualize your etheric body. You should have quite a bit of experience with this by now, so once you have this image firmly in your mind, see it begin to glow with a bright energy, usually white. As you see this, know that this energy is setting up a defensive force field around you and that no attacking energy can get through it. Continue to hold onto this image for as long as you can, and when it begins to fade let it go and relax.

It is at this point that your knowledge of psionics

comes in. You will remember the section on making circle patterns—not the amplifying patterns, but the ones that ended up with lines crisscrossing the interior of the circle. Go back to that section and follow the instructions to make a circle pattern that will correspond to the defensive field you have just built. With this pattern and your numerical gauge you can determine the relative strength of your defense. Meditate upon this waveform each night for at least a week, and after each meditation measure the strength of the pattern. Once it is over 80, you can relax and go on to other things, because the normal methods of psychic attack will not be able to penetrate it.

Once you have your basic field in place, you must determine if you really are under a psychic attack. After all, there is a difference between a threat and an action.

For this you will need a pendulum, a yes/no gauge like the one in *Psychic Power* (which I only recently learned is called an ideometer), and a trusted friend who can use the pendulum and will not call the men in the white coats when you ask him or her to do the small service for you. It is necessary to ask a friend, as you may not be able to be objective about the question. Have this friend hold the pendulum, and ask it for you if you really are under a psychic attack. If it says no, forget it. If it says yes, prepare your counterattack.

The simplest form of counterattack is to send the invading energy back to the attacker. In fact, this is the traditional method of psychic warfare, and it is the principal reason why, up to now, defense has always been more easy than attack. Let us face the fact that most psychics are not grounded in military history and know nothing of either fortification or siegecraft. Thus the attacking psychic would launch his or her assault hoping that his/her victim would not be able to defend against it, and the defender would only have to hide behind his/her field or circle and let the attacking energy bounce back at the attacker. The traditional methods used in launching such an attack are such that a psychic link always would exist between the invading force and the one who sent it. There is a relatively simple way around that, but we are not at that point yet.

If the attack took the form of a ritual, defense against it was even easier, for tradition required that such operations be carried out at a certain day and hour, and the defender, if he or she were versed in occult lore, would set up a strong defense at that time and let the assault bounce off. Thus if your enemy is using a ritual with such a tradition, you determine by using your pendulum when the attack will occur and at that time meditate upon your defense. In addition to that, place the circle pattern that you have made to correspond to your defensive field inside an amplifying pattern and turn on a light to shine on it. No traditional attack method has a chance against this defense.

But let us suppose that your enemy is attacking by other than a ritual method. Let us say that he or she has made a thoughtform that is designed to latch onto your ceiling and bathe your room with a continued feeling of anxiety. You will have to discover that the thoughtform is being used and then deal with it.

Make yourself a chart, and on this chart have a

space for "simple thought," "ritual," "ritual object," "thoughtform" and "psionic." These are the basic methods of psychic attack. You may also want to include a space marked "other," but it is not necessary. Hold your pendulum over the center of the chart and ask it what form of attack is being mounted. As we are considering a thoughtform offense now, let us assume that is where the pendulum has gone.

A thoughtform usually is fixed in one location and broadcasts from there, like the "psychic land mine" technique I taught you in *Psychic Power*, only here the purpose is not likely to be the harmless desire to make you like someone but rather to cause you some unpleasantness or even injury. This is what separates psychic combat from the usual run of psychic activity. A thoughtform has the advantage when used in attack in that it is very difficult to send back to its maker, for reasons which I will explain later, and its effects can be difficult to separate from the usual run-of-the-mill disasters that beset everyone. It can even be programmed to cause only certain results and thus can be very difficult to find. So first you should find it.

This is done by first making a circle pattern that will correspond to the attacking thoughtform. Once you have made such a pattern, set up your radionic box and take a rate for the thoughtform. Now begin to ask questions. First ask if the thoughtform is placed in your etheric body. Assuming that you get a negative response, begin to ask about likely locations, beginning with your room and working outward. Once you have a general location for the thoughtform, set up your helmet to the contact rate for that thoughtform. You need not worry about it influencing you any more than it already is, but by using some simple remote viewing procedures you can find the thoughtform and begin to work on it.

After you find the thoughtform, you must get an idea of its relative strength. This is done using the numerical gauge in the same way as you did to test your defensive field. Let us say that you get a strength reading of 76. This would make it an effective thought-form, but not a mighty one. Over 90 and you really must worry. Under 30 and you can dispose of it quite easily. This reading means that it has enough power to make balancing easy, but it is also a good idea to cut it off from its power source.

The thoughtform is balanced out of existence by using the same procedure you would in removing a waveform from your etheric body. You take a rate for the thoughtform and then set the dials to the balancing rate. This will attack the very nature of the thought-form, and by testing the strength of the thoughtform you will know when it is destroyed.

While you are doing this, you can starve the thoughtform by visualizing it as being encased in a shell with no opening, which will prevent all energy from its maker or the universe itself from reaching it. This procedure, when used in conjunction with the balancing method, will render the thoughtform non-existent in a short period of time.

Continue this defense until the thoughtform is exhausted. Now let us suppose that you do not know who your attacker is. Once the thoughtform has a power level under 40, you may safely use the pattern of the thoughtform to interrogate the thoughtform and learn who made it. After all, it is unlikely to have been created by a total stranger. You will need to know who to counterattack, and you do not wish to make a mistake in this regard. I remember one time, when I was young and inexperienced, I launched a powerful blast and it hit the wrong man. I was a very embarrassed young magician.

Assault by ritual object has a quaint ring about it, and it is so old a technique that it can be difficult to take seriously. For that very reason you should take it seriously, but you must avoid the usual extremes of making certain that no one has access to your hair clippings or fingernails. A truly experienced psychic warrior needs only a name, provided he or she knows the person. So the precautions of the more traditional occultist in this regard are foolish. Not only are they a waste of time, but they cause the person to look in the wrong direction, distracting him or her from the true menace. It is better to operate under the assumption that anyone who wishes can obtain a witness sample of you.

With that out of the way, you can begin to understand that ritual objects come in two varieties, at least for our purposes. First, there are those meant to be seen by the victim. This can mean anything from the charm taped to the front door or stuck in the mailbox to a knotted string jammed into the furniture. The second kind need never be seen by, or come near, the target, and this would be the sort of thing exemplified by the traditional voodoo doll. The first kind is rather amateurish and quite easily dealt with. All that is necessary is to put the thing on your radionic box and set up a balancing rate. After your gauge shows that its strength is gone, burn it. Of course, if your attacker knows that you are versed in psionics, he or she will probably not use such a crude technique.

The second type of object is a little more hard to deal with, but not overly so. As you will not have any direct contact with it, you will only feel its effect. In that regard, it is similar to a psionic assault. The difficulty, therefore, does not lie so much in the countering as in the finding.

You must first accurately determine that an attack is taking place. Remember, suspicion is not proof. After that, you must determine that the means of assault is a ritual object, in this case, let us say a doll. At this point you must understand that you are unlikely to get physical access to the doll if it has not been sent to you. So you must disregard as useless any instructions in other works that tell you how to physically destroy the thing. You are not going to be able to do that. What you must do is turn the energy of the doll back on the user.

Make a circle pattern of the doll and determine the power of its transmission. Now use the numerical gauge to learn the level of effect that the transmission is having on you. This will give you an idea of how serious the problem is. If you have a very low reading, you may wish to laugh the whole affair off and ignore it. If on the other hand you get a very high reading, you are going to have to do some work.

One of the reasons why no psychic warrior in his or her right mind will use a ritual object to attack an equally competent opponent is that the object may become as dangerous to the maker as to the intended victim. Think about it for a minute. The sorcerer puts a tremendous amount of effort into the making of such a thing. He or she must acquire the witness samples, find the proper materials, make the object and then go through the trouble of charging it. The object, in this case a doll, has become one hell of a witness for the attacker. You have a circle pattern that can function as a witness for the doll, therefore you have a link to the person who made it.

Now you can do a little ritual yourself. It is one of the few times when you will use such a thing with psionics, but the psychological power of it is enormous.

But first you must block the incoming energy. Using the circle pattern as a witness, find the balancing rate for the energy of the doll, as it affects you. Place a witness sample of yourself in the machine and let it go. That will knock out the attack. Now for the counter-blow.

Remember that most people who use charged objects in attack are not very bright, and it is quite possible, probable in fact, that the one who is striking at you will have neglected his or her own defenses. If he/she has not, I will teach you how to deal with that a little later, but for now let us assume that this is the case.

With your helmet, use the circle pattern and another radionic box to set up a contact rate for the sorcerer. You are balancing out the energy from the object, so you need not fear contacting it. Put on the helmet and try to see the object. This should be quite easy for you by now, but if not, a little practice will enable you to get a passable image. Now it gets just a bit harder. Try to see back in time to the point where the sorcerer was charging the object. I warn you, you may get some very unpleasant images, but hang on. While you are watching, hook the walkie-talkie into the end of the system. If you have to stop looking for a while to do this, it is no problem, for you will be able to return to the time with little trouble.

Keep watching the sorcerer. Now hit the on-button on the walkie-talkie and repeat the following:

> "Your evil magic and your black sorcery
> Are powerless to injure me.
> I give your curses back to thee.
> Return, return by three times three
> Return, I say, so mote it be."

What you have just done is taken the traditional means of returning a traditional curse and added one hell of a boost to it. It would be effective without psionics. With psionics, the results can be devastating.

In its most basic form a psionic attack can be relatively easy to halt. The weakness of psionics is that it can take a bit of time to work, so a disruption pattern aimed at you will not show its full effect until you are trying something important, and then everything will go wrong. The down side to this is that you may have no reason to suspect such an attack when it occurs.

The best defense, therefore, against a psionic attack is a psionic shield and a message thoughtform. The shield will slow down the effect of the attack, and the thoughtform will let you know if one is occurring. There is now a word of warning that I must give you. There are devices on the market that are advertised as being psionic shields. I have not personally tested any of them, and some of them may actually work, but I would be very hesitant about investing a lot of money into something that may be neutralized by a skilled opponent. You already have all the equipment that you may need.

A psionic shield is set up by taking a pattern that you feel may be most protective to you (see Appendix 2) and placing it in your standard box, taking a rate, recording the rate and then leaving the box at that rate with a witness of yourself. Sort of a radionic rabbit's foot, if you will. The incoming disruptive energy must contend with the helpful energy coming out of the box, and its effects are blunted, if not stopped completely. The only problem with this defense is that it takes up a machine and may only slow, but not stop, the attacking force.

Therefore you need to know if a psionic attack is on the way. For that you must make a special thought-form whose purpose is to inform you if there is an incoming psychic shell. You may make this form in any shape you find convenient and place it in your etheric body. It will have the basic command to cause you to dream of an attack the moment one occurs.

Let us assume that your thoughtform is in place, and one night you are awakened to see the smiling face of your worst enemy glaring out at you. Then you really wake up and discover that it was a very lifelike dream. The alarm has been sounded and you must go to war.

The first rule is to see to your defense. Have your friend use the pendulum to determine if the information given you was accurate. Assuming that it is, make a circle pattern for the incoming energy pattern. Take a rate for this pattern and balance it, with a witness of yourself in the machine. That will block the attack. And with any luck your opponent will not know the attack is blocked until you have successfully counterattacked.

You must counterattack. In psionic combat you cannot hide behind a shield indefinitely, because it is only a matter of time before the enemy realizes that his or her attack has failed and launches a new one, perhaps not directly at you but at someone close to you. The shield may also be neutralized by psionic means. Therefore you must view your defensive situation as temporary at best and set to work to counterattack.

So now it is time for you to learn the art of offensive action. Up to now we have more or less confined our study to simple sword and shield tactics. The attacker strikes and you defend, then you strike back. The time has come for a greater degree of sophistication in your methods.

In a very real sense psychic combat is a form of siege warfare. No attack can succeed unless it can penetrate the defensive system erected by the enemy. And this can be almost as difficult in psychic combat as it was in medieval warfare.

Begin your phase of the battle by laying some groundwork. You will want to counterattack with great force, so a prepared thoughtform is best. Begin to make such a thoughtform by visualizing it in the shape of some weapon, such as a bomb, and storing it somewhere your enemy is not likely to look for it if he or she should be using a remote-viewing technique to gather information. I have found that visualizing the thoughtform in a stationary orbit in outer space, like a satellite bomb, is a very good way to do this. At least three times a day—when you get up, after lunch and before bed—charge the thoughtform and keep a circle pattern of it in an amplifying pattern. Use your numerical gauge to study the level of its power, and do not stop charging until the gauge hits 90.

While you are doing this, take the time to perform a reconnaissance. If your opponent has an early-warning thoughtform like the one you used to detect his/her attack, you will want to disable it. The procedure here is the same as used in the thoughtform defense.

If you are able, get a witness sample of the enemy. You must be able to strike directly at him/her, for unlike the charged object counter, you cannot use his/her psionic device to attack him. A radionic box, when used to transmit a disruptive pattern, is powered not by the thought of the operator, as is normally assumed, but rather by the witness of the victim. This means that any energy the victim puts around or into the machine is shot back at him/her. For that reason, aside from balancing the incoming energy, there is no defense against a radionic attack. The only effect a traditional defense will have is to increase the power of the transmission from the box. You must attack the operator directly!

Let us assume that our enemy has been intelligent enough to surround him/herself with a defensive field. This can be done by directly placing it in his etheric body, as a waveform, or by creating a thoughtform that will continually transmit the protective waveform. This last is usually done by the method of creating a thoughtform over the head, which shines over the body.

Take the witness of the enemy and ask your pendulum if he or she has a defense. Then by asking questions, narrow down the nature of his/her defenses. Let us assume that he/she has a simple field defense that is not energized by a thoughtform.

Make a circle pattern that will correspond to the defensive field of the enemy. Place this pattern in a radionic box and take a rate for it. Now use your numerical gauge to learn its level of power. This last step is of great importance. Once you have done this, balance the rate for the enemy field. This will have the effect of slowly dissolving the defense of your opponent. It may take some time, especially if your opponent is in the habit of regularly charging his/her field, but you will dissolve it. You can lull an enemy into self-confidence by using your teleflasher and helmet set to a contact rate for him/her and every night as he/she sleeps sending the simple message "I won."

Regularly test the power level of the enemy field by using the numerical gauge. Once it has dropped below 30, you may prepare for the final assault.

Contact your thoughtform out in orbit. Give it one more instruction before the attack, and that instruction is to destroy itself if it does not achieve its purpose. This is of serious value, because you do not want your own thoughtform to be blasted back at you. Test the power level of the thoughtform one more time to be sure that it is high enough. A good technique to follow is to ask the numerical gauge the minimum power the thoughtform will need to penetrate the enemy's defense and fulfill its dread mission, and then ask the power of the thoughtform.

The battle is now ready for the final stage. It is roughly akin to having dug the final trench line and having brought up your siege cannon to virtually point-blank range against the besieged fortress.

Transfer the circle pattern of the thoughtform to a radionic box and take a contact rate for it. Set up your helmet by hooking it into the box and also taking a rate for the thoughtform. Place the witness of the enemy on a foil plate and hook that plate to the antenna of the walkie-talkie. Hook the walkie-talkie to the other end of the box. Put on the helmet. See your thoughtform floating in space. Give the command to attack and turn on the walkie-talkie. See the thoughtform shoot down from orbit and blast its way through the defense of the enemy and do its work. Keep watching your thoughtform for a short time, then break contact and take off the helmet. If you have an AC adaptor to your walkie-talkie, leave it on. If not, turn it off after twenty minutes and place the witness of the enemy on the receiving plate, or stick pad, of the box.

The above is really a very simplified version of combat between two experts at psionics. I have shortened it considerably for the purposes of this book. In real life, such a duel can go on for months, if not years—an elaborate chess game of move and counter-move, attack and counterattack, until one side either gives up or is defeated. But you should be able to see from the above why the traditional defense systems will fail against a psionic attack. It is not so much that they will be overpowered as that they will be simply removed. Such battle requires a knowledge not only of technique but also of timing, and the ability to coordinate several aspects of the battle at the same time.

The last piece of advice that I have to give you is not to place too much value on books that only teach psychic self-defense. If you are going to war, then you should study war and adapt the methods of psionic power to the broader principles of strategy. No one book, much less a single chapter of one, can tell you all that you must know. Therefore study well the history of combat and realize that though the weapons may change, the broad rules still apply.

This finishes another text on psionics and the power it can bring. I hope you will experiment on your own and use this as a text to build on, rather than as the final source of, all knowledge on the subject, which I can assure you it is not. Never view anything that I have written, or that anyone else has written, as all that can be learned about anything. We all make mistakes, and I have no doubt that some of what I have taught will be rendered obsolete with time. What is important is that we continue to search for truth and expand our knowledge of the universe. If we should crush a few toes or poleaxe some sacred cows along the way, then so be it. For as the saying has it, "There is no religion higher than truth."

APPENDIX 1
COUNTER-THOUGHTFORMING

Most people think of group meditation as being rather benign, and in most cases it is. There are, however, occasions when something goes wrong. When this happens it is the right, if not the responsibility, of the skilled operator to create a thoughtform that will negate the effect of the meditation.

To understand this, you must realize that in a group meditation two things are going on. First, a thoughtform is being created that will function according to the programming given it by the members of the group acting under the direction of the leader. Secondly, and of more importance, the process of meditation creates a mild trance, similar in effect to a light hypnotic state. While in such a state, the members of the group are easily directed in any way that the person leading the meditation wants to take them. If the meditation is being led by somebody who understands this, the risks become obvious.

With this fact in mind, you should never allow yourself to become part of group meditation unless you know the person leading it and you trust that person. My own practice in such situations is to look as if I am meditating with the group (after all, there is no point in hurting anyone's feelings unnecessarily) while maintaining my alertness. In this way, I never compromise my personal autonomy.

The result of remaining in a state of control is that you can watch the meditation, and if the leader invokes ideas that run counter to a value you hold strongly, you can visualize a thoughtform that will counter the one being created. Because of the Principle of Ultimate Instability, your thoughtform will be more coherent and thus more effective than the group's. If you know the situation in advance, as is often the case, you may even create a counter thoughtform and have it ready to bring out when needed.

As far as the thoughtform itself is concerned, that will depend on the nature of the one you are blocking. In general, your counter thoughtform will either attack the thoughtform itself or block its energy from the members of the group. Both work equally well, and the choice must be up to you. Like all other skills, with practice you will learn which technique works best for you.

APPENDIX 2
TRANSMITTAL PATTERNS FROM
THE LESSER KEY OF SOLOMON

One of the odd things about psionics is the fact that on rare occasions the more traditional aspects of magick intrude. The use of the 70 seals of various spirits in the *Lesser Key of Solomon* is such an instance. Normally used in ceremonial magick for the purpose of calling and controlling the spirits, these seals are also effective witnesses for certain patterns of energy that can be transmitted by means of a radionic box or amplifying pattern to a given subject.

It must be noted that when the seals are used in this manner, one does not assume that a given spirit is being contacted but that only a pattern of energy, possibly a thoughtform, associated with that spirit is being tapped. For that reason it would be most unwise to expect treasure to come floating into your living room because you have set up a rate for a spirit that is supposed to bring such things. In fact, the patterns often function in ways only slightly related to the usual behavior ascribed to the given spirits. The Gusion pattern, for example, is very good for getting through traffic. Therefore I suggest that you experiment with the patterns and discover for yourself what results you get and which patterns will best serve your purposes.

Agares

This is one of my favorite disruption patterns. It is supposed to be able to wreck careers and reduce the status of important people. The pattern works quite well on politicians. This pattern may also be able to cause earthquakes and increase the subject's knowledge of languages.

Aini

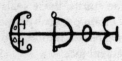

Another disruptive pattern, this one can cause fires, so it is said. It is more useful in improving the cleverness of the subject.

Allocen

I have not had much use for this pattern. It improves the ability to absorb knowledge, and would thus be extremely useful for a student, particularly of the natural sciences and astronomy.

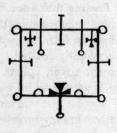

Amon

I highly recommend this pattern to my pacifist friends. It can reconcile friends and enemies and cause love.

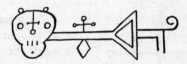

Amduscias

I was almost tempted to leave this one out. It is supposed to make trees fall and do little else, but you might like to try it on your weeds.

Amy

Transmit this one to your student friends. It is supposed to be quite helpful in learning.

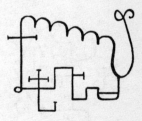

Andrealphus

Another student's helper, this one specializes in math.

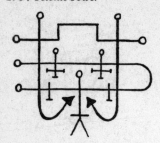

Andras

One of the most effective disruption patterns. HANDLE WITH CAUTION!

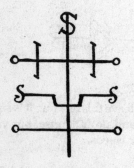

Andromalius

If you are having trouble dowsing for something, set up this pattern on your box with your own witness.

Asmoday

A useful pattern for dowsers and students. It increases abilities of both.

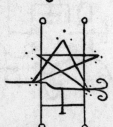

Astaroth

Another friend of the student, this pattern increases the ability to learn just about anything.

Baal

Not to be confused with the god of the Canaanites, this pattern increases learning ability.

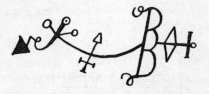

Balam

Another pattern for increasing knowledge. It is also supposed to aid in precognition and clairvoyance.

Barbatos

This pattern is useful for making friends, as well as for finding ways to make money.

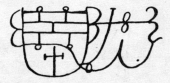

Bathin

This pattern increases the speed of travel. You might like to experiment and see if it cuts down your commuting time.

Beleth

The sole use of this pattern is to procure a mate. It is most effective when used with an amplifying pattern.

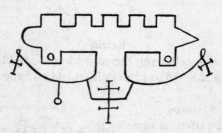

Belial

This pattern helps in any situation where it is necessary to gain the favor of others, particularly if you are running for office.

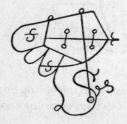

Berith

Another pattern useful in gaining promotions.

Bifrons

Where do they get these silly names? Anyway, this pattern is good for anyone studying mathematics.

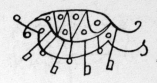

Botis

This pattern is good for turning enemies into friends. I must experiment and see if it works on critics.

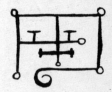

Buer

This is possibly the best pattern for general healing energy. Transmitting this pattern will help most illnesses. It is a favorite of mine.

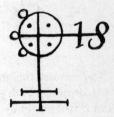

Bune

Transmit this pattern to anyone who is in financial difficulty or needs help with public speaking.

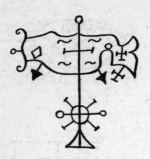

Caim

I must confess that I have never had much use for this pattern. It is supposed to help you understand animals, and our cats have never had any trouble making themselves understood.

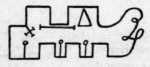

Cimeries

You can use this pattern to increase your courage and to improve both your knowledge of literature and your dowsing ability.

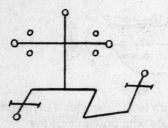

Dantalian

A good pattern for aid in remote viewing. It is also useful in making someone fond of you.

Decarabia

This is another pattern I have never had call to use. It is supposed to increase a person's knowledge of herbs and stones, two subjects I have never been much interested in.

Eligor

Now this is more my style. This pattern is useful for kindling lust and starting wars.

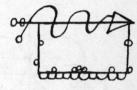

Flauros

Another extremely powerful disruption pattern. It is of particular use in psychic warfare.

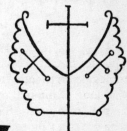

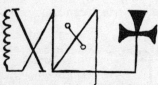

Focalor

This pattern looks almost like a circuit diagram, doesn't it? It is a disruption pattern that is most effective when used against shipping or for weather control.

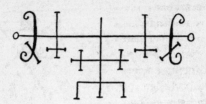

Foras

This pattern can help one master logic and become witty. I have never had much need of it myself.

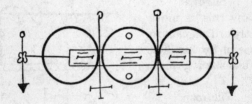

Forneus

Just for fun, I once showed this pattern to an electronics expert friend of mine, who immediately asked what kind of infernal machine I was building. Well, this pattern is just the thing if you or a friend happens to be taking a language course. It can also make your enemies your friends.

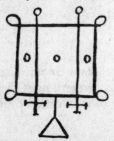

Furcas

Those who are having trouble with a philosophy course are strongly advised to use this pattern.

Furfur

This pattern helps cause love in marriage or thunder and lightning. You figure it out.

Gaap

This is a nice, general purpose pattern. It can be used to cause love or hate, increase divinatory skills and help with transportation problems.

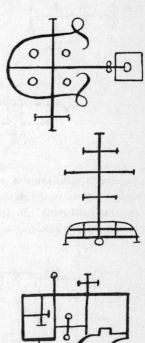

Gamygyn

A pattern for those who wish to contact the dead.

Glasyalabolas

The energies of this pattern incite men to violence and murder. Just the thing for a family reunion.

Gomory

This pattern is useful in gaining the love of women. I don't know if it works on men.

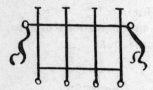

Gusion

Another favorite pattern of mine. It reconciles enemies, causes honor and promotion, and works wonders at getting through traffic.

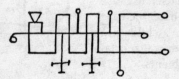

Hagenti

There is little known use for this pattern, so you might want to experiment with it. The spirit was supposed to turn metal into gold or wine into water, two abilities of dubious modern value.

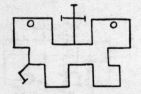

Halpas

This is another disruptive pattern.

Ipos

Aim this pattern at yourself if you need either wit or courage.

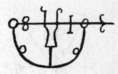

Lerajie

This is a disruption pattern, the function of which is the exact opposite of the Buer pattern. It delays healing.

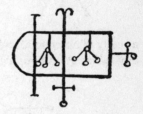

Malpas

Another disruption pattern.

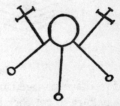

Marbas

You may use this pattern in all matters regarding health, either to improve healing or to cause illness.

Marchosias

Transmit this pattern to yourself if you are about to engage in any sort of combat.

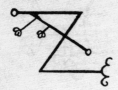

Morax

Transmit this one to your favorite astrologer. He or she might give you an accurate reading for once.

Murmur

This pattern is useful to those who wish to contact the dead that have been gone for some time. However, if they have been gone too long, they may have already reincarnated, and thus you should be wary of any information you might receive.

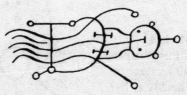

Naberius

If you have managed to get your boss mad at you, use this pattern to get back in his or her good graces.

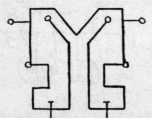

Orias

Another pattern useful for gaining promotions.

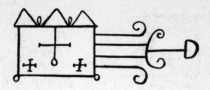

Orobas
This pattern, too, is useful in gaining friends and influence.

Ose
This pattern, when beamed at an opponent, can seriously inhibit his or her reasoning abilities.

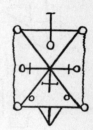

Paimon
If you wish to have power over people, and that is what much of this book is about, use this pattern.

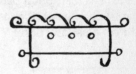

Phoenix
This pattern should be used if you wish to write poetry but cannot get your rhyme and meter straight.

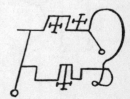

Procel

If your local adolescent is having trouble with geometry, give him or her a shot of this pattern and his/her grades should improve.

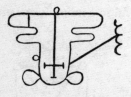

Purson

Set up this pattern before you go dowsing for something valuable. It helps.

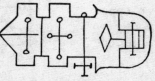

Raum

This is a disruption pattern that is useful not only against people but cities as well. Keep it in mind after you get a parking ticket.

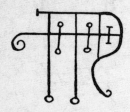

Ronobe

Another pattern that is most useful for making friends.

Sabnack

This is a disruption that is specifically effective against shipping, or anything else pertaining to the sea.

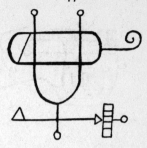

Saleos

All this pattern does is promote attraction between the sexes. That seems to be enough.

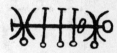

Seere

Here is another pattern that needs experimenting with. The spirit it was supposed to represent had the useful ability of causing anything to happen, which covers a lot of territory.

Shax

This pattern can be used either to bring money or as a disruption pattern.

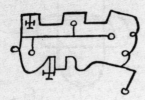

Solas

Anyone who is a student of astronomy, astrology, or herbalism would do well to take an occasional dose of this pattern.

Sytry

Another erotic pattern, this one will stimulate attraction between any man or woman.

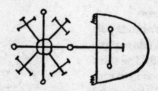

Valac

This pattern is of use only if you are a snake charmer who is looking for treasure, because it can give a person power over reptiles and help dowse for wealth.

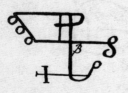

Valefor

This pattern is a good healing pattern for all ills except kleptomania, because it can also be used to create a desire to steal. It is therefore not a good pattern to transmit to a politician.

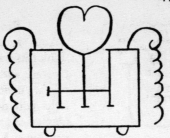

Vapula

No, this is not a valentine for a mad scientist. This pattern is useful to any student, for it increases knowledge.

Vassago

In addition to being the only pattern with feet, this pattern increases the abilities of dowsers and remote viewers.

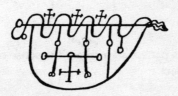

Vepar

Another disruptive pattern, this one has its province in the water and can be used to attack shipping, fishermen, swimmers, etc. It can also be used to hinder healing.

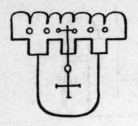

Vine

You would almost think this pattern was created with psychic warfare in mind. It can help you dowse the identity of an attacking psychic and penetrate his or her defenses.

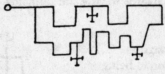

Vual

After the war is over, you can use this pattern to patch things up. It causes friendship.

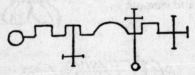

Zagan

Use this pattern to increase the sense of humor of your subject.

Zepar

After some of the patterns in this catalog, it is pleasant to end with one whose sole ability is to cause love.

APPENDIX 3
MAGICK SQUARES OF
THE SEVEN PLANETS

Nowhere is the relationship between psionics and magick closer than in the use of transmittal patterns made from planetary magick squares. The planet whose influence is used is chosen in the same way that it would be in a traditional magickal operation. Once that is decided, the pattern is made from the square and placed in the transmittal end of the radionic box or, if the pattern represents a thoughtform to be charged, in the center of an amplifying pattern.

The influence of the planets is as follows:

Saturn: any disruptive activity, any attempt to increase knowledge

Jupiter: wealth, promotion, friendship, health

Mars: acquiring courage, disruption

Sun: wealth, health, friendship, anything positive

Venus: love in all its forms

Mercury: increasing intelligence, business matters, knowledge

Moon: travel, love, any operation involving water

Saturn

4	9	2
3	5	7
8	1	6

Mars

11	24	7	20	3
4	12	25	8	16
17	5	13	21	9
10	18	1	14	22
23	6	19	2	15

Jupiter

4	14	15	1
9	7	6	12
5	11	10	8
16	2	3	13

Sun

6	32	3	34	35	1
7	11	27	28	8	30
19	14	16	15	23	24
18	20	22	21	17	13
25	29	10	9	26	12
36	5	33	4	2	31

Venus

22	47	16	41	10	55	4
5	23	43	17	42	11	29
30	6	24	49	18	36	12
13	31	7	25	13	19	37
38	14	32	1	26	44	20
21	39	8	33	2	27	45
46	15	40	9	34	3	28

Mercury

8	58	59	5	4	62	63	1
49	15	14	52	53	11	10	56
41	23	22	44	45	19	18	48
32	34	35	29	28	38	39	25
40	26	27	37	36	30	31	33
17	47	46	20	21	43	42	24
9	55	54	12	13	51	50	16
64	2	3	61	60	6	7	57

Moon

37	78	29	70	21	62	13	54	5
6	38	79	30	71	22	65	14	46
47	7	39	80	31	72	23	55	56
16	48	8	40	81	32	64	24	56
57	17	49	9	41	73	33	65	25
26	58	18	50	1	42	74	34	66
67	27	59	10	51	2	43	75	35
36	68	19	60	11	52	3	44	76
77	28	69	20	61	12	53	4	45

APPENDIX 4
BASIC RADIONICS

This appendix is for those of you who have not had the good luck to be acquainted with my first book and thus have not had the opportunity to build the psionic devices that are so necessary to the mastery of this art; for just as the magician cannot function without his or her wand and sword, neither can one who intends to practice psionics hope to achieve any results without certain basic machinery.

To begin with, you will need a pendulum. There are any number of commercial pendulums on the market, mostly overpriced, but you can make one quite simply by using a weight (an old key works very nicely) and a convenient length of string. If you wish to make a good one, a child's wooden top is the best. Take the top and insert a screw-eye into the flat end. All that is necessary now is to attach your string, and you will have a very good and accurate pendulum, as shown in Figure 20. This is the type that I have used for some years now.

Make a chart as in Figure 21. This chart will answer three ways: "yes," "no," and "no information." You can determine which answer is which by holding the pendulum over the center of the cross-lines and asking it to swing for each answer. Then mark on the

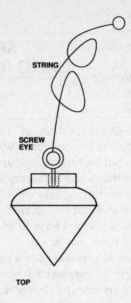

Figure 20

chart the direction of the swing. Usually the device will swing forward and back for yes, side to side for no, and around the circle if there is no information. Because the pendulum reveals how your own nervous system responds, do not be upset if it chooses to answer by circling counterclockwise for no and clockwise for yes. The pendulum, like the operator, is a very individual thing, and it may take some practice to get to know how to use it.

The radionic devices themselves take a bit of work to make and use, but they are far easier to work with than it may seem at first look. For your box (see

Figure 22) you will need

    one metal can

    one plastic lid from a coffee can or can of cat food

    three potentiometers (volume control things) available at any electronics store

    three knobs

    two jacks

    unshielded copper wire (usually called magnet wire)

    hook-up wire

    (The resistance of the wire and the potentiometers is not important, because the energies we use, while related to electricity, are not in themselves electromagnetic.)

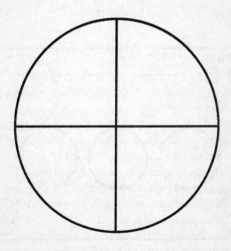

Figure 21

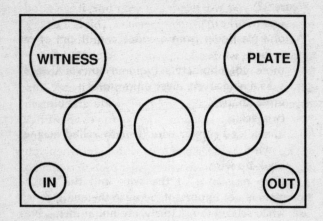

Figure 22

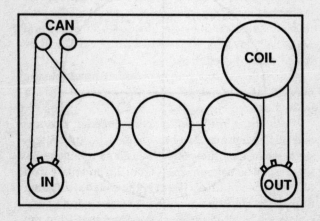

Figure 23

Before you begin to make your box, it is a good idea to learn how to use the stick pad. This is the plastic lid. Lay the lid on a table and rub your thumb very lightly over it while asking yourself an obvious question, such as, "Is $2+2=4$?" You should notice a distinct difference in feeling from the thumb, and it may stop altogether, almost as if the plastic were grabbing it. When you get the reaction, you have a yes answer. A negative reaction (no response after a few rubs) means no. Play with the stick pad for a while, and when you can get a good reaction on a regular basis, it is time to build your radionic box.

The box is wired as you can see from Figure 22. A cardboard box makes a nice cheap cabinet and has the advantage that it is easy to punch holes in.

Begin by laying out on the box where you will have everything go. This may seem obvious, but you will be amazed at how even an author can become embarrassed by forgetting this simple step. Make the holes for the can, the jacks, the potentiometers and two small holes for the magnet wire, which will be coiled under the stick pad.

Take the can and punch two small holes into the bottom. Insert two small screws in these and attach it to the box (see Figure 24).

Wire the three potentiometers together in series and attach them to the box. Then wire the potentiometer nearest the can to the can as in Figure 23. Make a coil of magnet wire (Figure 25) and place it on top of the box, with each end of the coiled wire going through the hole assigned to it. Wire one end of that coil to the potentiometer at the other end from the first, and attach the other end of the magnet wire to the

Figure 24 Witness Sample Container

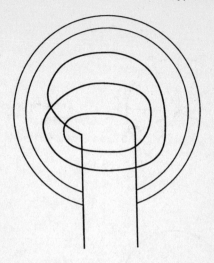

Figure 25 Detector Plate

can. This will make a complete circuit between the can, the potentiometers and the coil.

Insert the first jack in the hole under the can, and wire it to the can as shown in Figure 23. Repeat the procedure with the other jack and the coil.

All that now remains is to attach the knobs to the potentiometers. If you have knobs that are already calibrated, set each one at zero directly over the top of the dial position, and mark the box at that point. If they are not calibrated, it is easy to calibrate them. Measure the distance around the circle that each knob travels and then divide that off so that each knob is moving between numbers zero and ten. An easy way to do this is to make a circle on a piece of paper and, using a

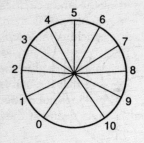

Draw circle and divide

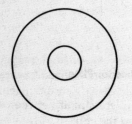

Cut hole in center of circle

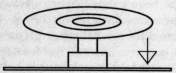

Glue circle over box so that the potentiometer stem fits through it

Figure 26

protracter and ruler, divide it off. Then make smaller circles divided the same way, using the larger circle as a pattern. Place those over the potentiometer stem, and glue each one in place before attaching the knobs (see Figure 26).

Once the knobs are on and calibrated, glue the plastic lid over the coil, making sure that the coil is completely under the lid. It probably does not matter if a wire is sticking out, but it looks neater if they do not.

Now that you have your box, you must learn to use it. The can is used for what is called a witness sample. This can be anything from the person whom you wish to contact or influence, such as a photograph or signature. In practical terms, these are the only witness samples that you are likely to obtain, so ignore what anyone else says about hair or fingernail clippings, and forget about blood and saliva. A witness sample is your link to that person, and the machine will act on the person through the witness.

Once you have the witness sample in the can, take what is called a contact rate for the person. A rate is the reading on the dials after you have set the machine, and it is called a contact rate because this particular rate puts you in clear, psychic contact with the person. This is done by first clearing your mind as much as possible and then turning each dial (starting from zero) slowly while you rub the stick pad. Once you get a stick on the pad, you have the rate for that dial, and you repeat the procedure with each dial until all three dials have been set.

Once you have done this, place the box where you can rest the palm of your left hand on the stick pad while holding your pendulum over the chart you have made. With this arrangement, ask the pendulum to tell you something that you do not already know about the subject. When you do this, the box helps cut through much of the noise that often interferes with psychic accuracy.

At this point you may wish to make a new chart for the pendulum, one which will allow it to spell out words. To do this, make a large half-circle on a piece of paper and mark it off with a space for each letter, numbers from zero to nine, and certain punctuation marks, such as a comma and a period.

By using this chart and the contact rate, you can gain much information that would otherwise not be available to you. There is only one weakness in the system that you must be aware of. If you are emotionally involved in the answer, you will get the answer you want rather than the true one, so try to keep your questions to matters about which you are disinterested.

The next tool you will need is the portable detector. This handy little gadget can be used to replace the pendulum in some cases and has other uses as well, as you will find out in this book.

As you can see from Figure 27, this is nothing more than a modification of the stick pad. To make it you will need

> one plastic lid
> one six-foot length of speaker wire (from the same electronics store where you bought the potentiometers)
> one plug (mono), which should be the same size as the jacks on your box
> One length of magnet wire

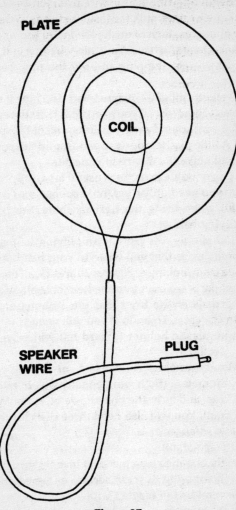

Figure 27

Begin by stripping the wire from the ends of the speaker wire, then split the insulated ends so that you have about one inch of unshielded wire and one inch of slack. Once you have done this, wire one end of the speaker wire to the plug and put the plug back together.

Make a coil of the magnet wire and tape it under the plastic lid. Now all you need do is twist the ends of the coil wire around each remaining end of the speaker wire. A little plastic tape wrapped around this connection will make the device look neater.

The portable detector is useful for any operation where you need only a yes/no response, and is quite helpful when using the next machine, the psionic amplifying helmet.

Put simply, the psionic amplifying helmet is a radionic device that you wear on your head. As you can see from looking at Figures 28 and 29, all the component parts are built into the helmet itself, with the tuning dials at the front and the antenna encased within the crest. To build it you will need

> one plastic helmet (a hard hat will work perfectly)
> three variable condensers or three potentiometers (both work equally well in rate taking, and as in the box, the value is not important. You will also need three dials for them.)
> one small jack
> a piece of foil
> eight one-inch long pieces of magnet strip (usually found in the craft section of dimestores)
> several feet of magnet wire
> hook-up wire

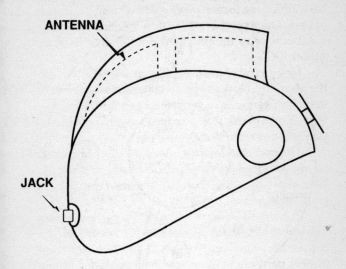

Figure 28

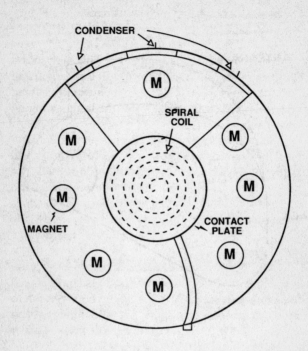

Figure 29

a sheet of one-half inch styrofoam
duct tape

Begin by trying the helmet on. This may sound silly, but as everything will have to fit inside, you will want it to be comfortable, without constantly having your hair stuck with the wires or the tuners banging your forehead.

Look at the front and find the center of the forehead, high enough so that the works of the tuner will be totally inside the helmet and the dials will not scrape the rim. Mark this point and measure around each side of it a couple of inches so that when the dials are mounted they will form a nice row across the front. Actually the dials can be anywhere, but this way the helmet looks nice.

At this point you should decide where you are going to put the jack. In my illustrations I have placed the jack at the back of the head, but you may wish to have it at the side. That's fine, but remember that you do not want it to be scraping against your head or cheek. Mark the spot for this as well.

The last mark goes at the top of the helmet, in the center. That is where the antenna wire comes out.

Once this is done, take the helmet out to the garage and hook up your drill, but before you make any holes, be sure to measure not only the stems and screws of the jack and condensers but also the nuts that will hold them on.

Once the holes are drilled, wire the condensers in series as you did in making your box, and mount them on the helmet.

Take your pieces of magnet strip and mount them

inside the helmet. As you mount them, make sure that the polarities of each strip alternate. Magnet strip works a little differently from the usual bar magnet, which actually makes this task easier, for all you have to do is stick them on in an alternating horizontal and vertical pattern, so that if the magnet at the front is vertical, the magnets on each side of it will be horizontal. Try to keep them an equal distance apart.

If the helmet has a removable liner, I assume that you have had the sense to remove it before the above operations. Put it back in and see how it fits, then take it out again. Cut the foil into a circle and fix this so that when the liner is in, the foil will press directly on the top of the head, right over the crown chakra. If you do not have a removable liner, go on to the next paragraph.

If you do not have a liner, make the coil with the unshielded wire, saving enough for the antenna. If you have not cut the foil circle, do it now.

Mount this coil under the center hole in the top of the helmet. If you have a liner, wire the coil to the foil circle, and if you do not, place the circle over the ends of the wire and glue it in place.

Insert the jack. If the jack has three tabs, attach the wires to the two outside ones and ignore the center one. Make sure that the wires from the jack are long enough so that they will not interfere with your head, and attach the other ends to the circle with a drop of solder. Now wire the condensers to the circle as shown in Figure 29.

All you need to do now is make the crest and antenna.

Begin by making the crest first. It is a little complicated, so pay close attention.

Start by cutting the styrofoam sheet into two equal pieces. Put these aside and make a pattern from a sheet of paper.

Tape the paper down to a table and rest the helmet on its side so that the top of the helmet is parallel to the paper. Trace the curve of the helmet on the paper and then set the helmet aside. Lift the paper from the table and cut out the curved section. Now test it to see that it fits the top of the helmet. Get this right! The crest must fit properly. It can be frustrating, but it is very important.

Once you have this pattern, draw the complete crest on it so that it will look like Figure 28. Carefully cut each piece of styrofoam so that it fits the pattern, and try each piece on the helmet.

Cut the wire for the antenna and lay it along the side of one of the pieces of the crest, making certain that the ends of the wire come out from under the crest. Spread glue and lay the other half of the crest on top, allowing it to harden. Once it is hard, either attach the wires to the circle of foil if the helmet has a liner or twist them to the wires coming out of the top. Once this last connection is made, glue the crest to the top of the helmet.

Neatly wrap the crest in duct tape to protect the styrofoam. Attach the dials to the tuners and paint the helmet red, except for the dials. (It is proven that wearing red on the head increases psychic output.)

You should now acquire a patch cable so that you can attach the helmet to your box. You will remember that the box has two jacks. The jack attached to the can is for input, and the jack attached to the coil is for output, so if you wish to transmit to the subject on the box, you would plug the helmet into the jack under the can, and if you wish to receive from the subject, you would attach the helmet to the jack under the stick pad.

The helmet is tuned by placing a witness sample in front of you, inserting the plug from the portable detector into the jack, and turning the dials while rubbing the plate. Alternatively, the helmet can be attached to the box and a contact rate taken on both using the stick pad on the box.

The helmet is used primarily in communication work, and to aid in psychic transmission you will need a deceptively simple device called a teleflasher. To make this machine you will need

one cardboard box
one lightbulb socket and wire set
one 25-watt lightbulb
one flasher plug

Begin by cutting out the bottom of the box. When doing this, cut a nice rectangle out of the cardboard so that you will have a piece to use for the back support. Make a hole in the side of the box and insert the socket for the lightbulb, and screw the bulb in (see Figure 30). Attach the flasher plug to the plug of the socket set. Now bend the remaining piece of cardboard so that it will stand up, and glue it to the box so that the light will shine up through the hole in the box and onto the cardboard. Plug in the light and test it. The bulb should glow weakly for a few seconds and then flash on and off with some degree of regularity. This device is used in dim light, so if the light coming out of

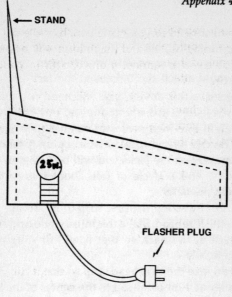

← STAND

25w.

FLASHER PLUG

Figure 30

the hole in the box is too bright, then you may cover it with a piece of translucent plastic or sheet of wax paper.

When using the teleflasher, the word or picture that you wish to transmit is placed standing against the back support and the light turned on. As you look at it, the flashing light will aid in the sending of the message by the psychic capacity of your brain. When used with the aid of a radionic box and a psionic amplifying helmet, the message hits the subject with tremendous power.

If making the psionic amplifying helmet seems to be too intimidating a task (and it was for me at first), a simple headband can be made which, while not having the tuning function of the helmet, will nevertheless enable you to connect yourself to the machines in this book.

To make this device, you will need two longish strips of posterboard, about one and one-half inches wide, eight one-inch pieces of magnet strip, several feet of double strand speaker wire, a plug (preferably the same size as the jacks you will be using on your machines) and a circle of foil, about two to three inches in diameter.

Begin by sizing the first strip to fit around your head at the forehead. Make this into a circle, and staple or glue it at the back so that it will fit snugly, yet not too tightly.

Now size the overhead strip so that it runs from the center of your forehead to the center of the back. When worn, the strap over the head will keep the headband from slipping down, so that band need not be too tight.

Punch two holes in the top strap at the point where it covers the top of your head, the location of the crown chakra. Now place the magnet strip around the headband, alternating the polarities, as shown in Figure 31.

Attach the plug to one end of the wire and strip the insulation off the other ends of the wire. Put these ends through the two holes in the top and spread the wire in opposite directions. Glue the foil circle in place over the wire so that it will rest on the crown chakra, as shown in Figure 32.

In use, the headband is simply worn and the wire plugged into the radionic box. The arrangement of the magnets automatically tunes it when you face north. This device is also useful in very hot weather when you simply do not wish to be burdened with the weight of the helmet.

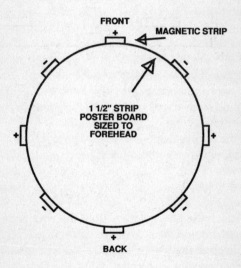

Figure 31

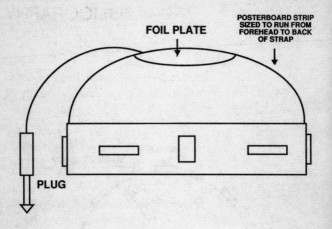

FOIL PLATE

POSTERBOARD STRIP SIZED TO RUN FROM FOREHEAD TO BACK OF STRAP

PLUG

Figure 32

SELECT
BIBLIOGRAPHY

Allen, Phil; Bearne, Alastair; and Smith, Roger. *Energy, Matter and Form*. Boulder Creek, CA: University of the Trees Press, 1979.

Beasley, Victor. *Your Electro-Vibratory Body*. Boulder Creek, CA: University of the Trees Press, 1979.
———. *Subtle Body Healing*. Boulder Creek, CA: University of the Trees Press, 1979.

Bentov, Itzhak. *Stalking the Wild Pendulum*. New York: E. P. Dutton, 1977.

Boswell, Harriet A. *Master Guide to Psychism*. New York: Lancer Books, 1969.

Cosimano, Charles W. *Psychic Power*. St. Paul, MN: Llewellyn, 1987.

Day, Langston. *Matter in the Making*. London: Vincent Stuart, 1966.

Leadbeater, Charles W. *The Chakras*. Chicago: Theosophical Publishing House, 1927.
———. *Clairvoyance*. Wheaton, IL: Theosophical Publishing House, 1967.
———. *The Inner Life*. Wheaton, IL: Theosophical Publishing House, 1978.

Phillips, Steven M. *Extrasensory Perception of Quarks.* Wheaton, IL: Theosophical Publishing House, 1980.

_____. "Extrasensory Perception of Subatomic Particles." *Fate* magazine, April, 1987, pp. 82-91.

_____. "Extrasensory Perception of Subatomic Particles." *Fate* magazine, May, 1987, pp. 82-92.

Regardie, Israel. *How to Make and Use Talismans.* New York: Samuel Weiser, 1972.

Smith, Michael G. *Crystal Power.* St. Paul, MN: Llewellyn, 1985.

Tansley, David V. *Chakras—Rays and Radionics.* Saffron Walden, UK: C. W. Daniel, 1985.

_____. *Dimensions of Radionics.* Devon, UK: Health Science Press, 1977.

_____. *Radionics and the Subtle Anatomy of Man.* Whitstable, UK: Health Science Press, 1972.

Waite, Arthur Edward. *The Book of Ceremonial Magic.* New York: Citadel, 1971.

STAY IN TOUCH

On the following pages you will find listed, with their current prices, some of the books and tapes now available on related subjects. Your book dealer stocks most of these, and will stock new titles in the Llewellyn series as they become available. We urge your patronage.

To obtain a FREE COPY of our latest full CATALOG of New Age books, tapes, videos, crystals, products and services, just write to the address below. In each 80 page catalog sent out bimonthly, you will find articles, reviews, the latest information on New Age topics, a listing of news and events, and much more. It is an exciting and informative way to stay in touch with the New Age and the world. The first copy will be sent free of charge and you will continue receiving copies as long as you are an active customer. You may also subscribe to *The Llewellyn New Times* by sending a $2.00 donation ($7.00 for Canada & Mexico, and $20.00 for overseas). Order your copy of *The Llewellyn New Times* today!

The Llewellyn New Times
P.O. Box 64383-Dept. 096, St. Paul, MN 55164

TO ORDER BOOKS AND PRODUCTS
ON THE FOLLOWING PAGES:

If your book dealer does not carry the titles and products listed on the following pages, you may order them directly from Llewellyn. Just write us a letter. Please add $2 for postage and handling for orders of $10 and under. Orders over $10 require $3.50 postage and handling. (USA and in US funds). UPS Delivery: We ship UPS whenever possible. Delivery guaranteed. Provide your street address as UPS does not deliver to P.O. Boxes; UPS to Canada requires a $50 minimum order. Allow 4-6 weeks for delivery. Orders outside the USA and Canada: Airmail—add $5 per book; add $3 for each non-book item (tapes, etc.); add $1 per item for surface mail.

Send orders to:

LLEWELLYN PUBLICATIONS
P.O. Box 64383-096
St. Paul, MN 55164-0383, U.S.A.

PSYCHIC POWER
by Charles Cosimano

Although popular in many parts of the world, *Radionics* machines have had little application in America, *UNTIL NOW!* Charles Cosimano's book, *Psychic Power*, introduces these machines to America with a new purpose: to increase your psychic powers! Using the easy, step-by-step instructions, and for less than a $10.00 investment, you can build a machine which will allow you to read other people's minds, influence their thoughts, communicate with their dreams and be more successful when you do divinations such as working with Tarot cards or Pendulums.

If you just want a book to read, you will find this a wonderful title to excitingly fill a few hours. But if you can spare a few minutes to actually build and use these devices, you will be able to astound yourself and your friends. We are not talking about guessing which numbers will come up on a pair of dice at a mark slightly above average. With practice, you will be able to choose which numbers will come up more often than not! But don't take our word for it. Read the book, build the devices and find out for yourself.

0-87542-097-4, 224 pages, mass market, illus. $3.95

THE LLEWELLYN PRACTICAL GUIDE
TO PSYCHIC SELF-DEFENSE AND WELL-BEING
by Denning & Phillips

Psychic well-being and Psychic self-defense are two sides of the same coin—just as physical health and resistance to disease are: each person (and every living thing) is surrounded by an electro-magnetic force field, or AURA, that can provide the means to psychic self-defense and to dynamic well-being. This book explores the world of very real "psychic warfare" that we all are victims of.

This book shows the nature of genuine psychic attacks—ranging from actual acts of black magic to bitter jealousy and hate—and the reality of psychic stress. It shows how each person must develop his weakened aura into a powerful defense-shield—thereby gaining both physical protection and energetic well-being that can extend to protection from physical violence, accidents . . . even ill-health.

0-87542-190-3, 288 pgs., 5¼ x 8, illus., softcover $7.95